Flourishing in Music Education

Flourishing in Music Education: Lessons from Positive Psychology presents research, theory, and best practices about potential pitfalls, as well as strategies for how successful music teachers can negotiate issues in the wake of the COVID-19 climate, both on a daily and long-term basis.

Masked and physically distanced classes have been particularly challenging for studio practice and group rehearsals, leading to virtual and digitally edited performances. This concise book is an essential read for those faced with such challenges, addressing key topics including engagement, relationships, meaning, accomplishment, resilience, and hope. Readers are provided with vignettes of struggling and successful music educators, which are then used to examine and consider new techniques and classic reminders for healthy enjoyment of work and life.

H. Christian Bernhard II, Ph.D., is Professor of Music Education at The State University of New York at Fredonia, where he teaches undergraduate courses in instrumental music methods and rehearsal techniques, as well as graduate courses in music education history, philosophy, psychology, assessment, and curriculum.

Routledge New Directions in Music Education Series
Series Editor: Clint Randles

The **Routledge New Directions in Music Education Series** consists of concise monographs that attempt to bring more of the wide world of music, education, and society into the discourse in music education.

Eco-Literate Music Pedagogy
Daniel J. Shevock

The Music Profiles Learning Project
Let's Take This Outside
Radio Cremata, Gareth Dylan Smith, Joseph Michael Pignato, and Bryan Powell

A Different Paradigm in Music Education
Re-examining the Profession
David A. Williams

Eudaimonia
Perspectives for Music Learning
Edited by Gareth Dylan Smith and Marissa Silverman

Managing Stress in Music Education
Routes to Wellness and Vitality
H. Christian Bernhard II

Meanings of Music Participation
Scenarios from the United States
Edited by C. Victor Fung and Lisa J. Lehmberg

Flourishing in Music Education
Lessons from Positive Psychology
H. Christian Bernhard II

Flourishing in Music Education
Lessons from Positive Psychology

H. Christian Bernhard II

NEW YORK AND LONDON

First published 2023
by Routledge
605 Third Avenue, New York, NY 10158

and by Routledge
4 Park Square, Milton Park, Abingdon, Oxon, OX14 4RN

Routledge is an imprint of the Taylor & Francis Group, an informa business

© 2023 H. Christian Bernhard II

The right of H. Christian Bernhard, II to be identified as author of this work has been asserted in accordance with sections 77 and 78 of the Copyright, Designs and Patents Act 1988.

All rights reserved. No part of this book may be reprinted or reproduced or utilised in any form or by any electronic, mechanical, or other means, now known or hereafter invented, including photocopying and recording, or in any information storage or retrieval system, without permission in writing from the publishers.

Trademark notice: Product or corporate names may be trademarks or registered trademarks, and are used only for identification and explanation without intent to infringe.

Library of Congress Cataloging-in-Publication Data
Names: Bernhard, H. Christian, II author.
Title: Flourishing in music education: lessons from positive psychology / H. Christian Bernhard II.
Description: [1.] | New York: Routledge, 2022. | Series: Routledge new directions in music education series | Includes bibliographical references and index.
Identifiers: LCCN 2022021212 (print) | LCCN 2022021213 (ebook) | ISBN 9781032362854 (hardback) | ISBN 9781032362878 (paperback) | ISBN 9781003331148 (ebook)
Subjects: LCSH: Music – Instruction and study – Psychological aspects. | COVID-19 Pandemic, 2020 – Social aspects. | Positive psychology.
Classification: LCC MT1.B544 F56 2022 (print) | LCC MT1.B544 (ebook) | DDC 780.71 – dc23/eng/20220429
LC record available at https://lccn.loc.gov/2022021212
LC ebook record available at https://lccn.loc.gov/2022021213

ISBN: 978-1-032-36285-4 (hbk)
ISBN: 978-1-032-36287-8 (pbk)
ISBN: 978-1-003-33114-8 (ebk)

DOI: 10.4324/9781003331148

Typeset in Times New Roman
by Apex CoVantage, LLC

To all of my teachers and students, with gratitude for every lesson learned.

Contents

	Series Foreword	viii
1	Space and Grace	1
2	Positive Emotion	8
3	Engagement	18
4	Relationships	28
5	Meaning	39
6	Accomplishment	49
7	Resilience	59
8	Hope	68
	Index	78

Series Foreword

The Routledge New Directions in Music Education Series consists of concise monographs that attempt to bring more of the wide world of music, education, and society – and all of the conceptualizations and pragmatic implications that come with that world – into the discourse of music education. It is about discovering and uncovering big ideas for the profession, criticizing our long-held assumptions, suggesting new courses of action, and putting ideas into motion for the prosperity of future generations of music makers, teachers of music, researchers, scholars, and society.

Clint Randles, Series Editor

1 Space and Grace

Times are tough. Teachers are frustrated, administrators are tired, and education majors wonder whether they should change career paths. A recent article (Perna, 2022) has been spreading quickly on social media, in which the author states that almost half of teachers in the United States have strongly considered resigning in the past 30 days. This past week, two local school districts announced a four-day weekend due to lack of available teachers and staff. The COVID-19 pandemic continues to create uncertainly (most recently with the rapidly spreading Omicron variant), school violence (both real and rumored) still presents unrest and tension, and teachers feel undervalued by politicians and other members of the community (Perna, 2022).

DOI: 10.4324/9781003331148-1

2 *Space and Grace*

The situation is particularly difficult for music teachers, both pre-service and in-service, due to a long-standing sense of inferiority. When administrators and other school leaders seek reform, they tend to focus on core subjects like English language and math, treating music ensembles and classes as extras that may or may not fit the traditional school day, particularly during times of uncertainty (Jennings, 2021). The challenges for music educators during the pandemic have only been magnified by concern over virus spread via traditional activities like singing, playing wind instruments, and combining large numbers of students for ensemble performance. Miksza et al. (2021) supported these observations through descriptive research. They surveyed 2,023 PK–12 and collegiate music teachers at the beginning of the COVID-19 pandemic and found that participants reported significantly lower levels of overall well-being and significantly higher levels of depression than published norms.

Teacher stress and burnout were a topic of research and concern even before COVID-19. Christina Maslach and her colleagues began studying educator burnout in the 1970s and '80s (e.g., Maslach et al., 1983), and numerous others have been investigating music educator stress for the past several decades (e.g., Bernhard, 2005, 2016; Conway et al., 2005; Gilbert, 2021; Hamann, 1986; Nápoles, 2022; Parkes et al., 2021; Roseth, 2019). Jennings (2021) suggested that the problem is much more complicated than just tired teachers in need of a pep talk. She convincingly argued for systemic change within the profession, outlining why practices dating from the Industrial Revolution of the 1800s are bound to fail within current social norms. She stated:

> I believe that today our school systems need to transition from the monocultural factory system, designed to promote standardization, to a permaculture model that values and promotes all forms of diversity, such as race, culture, behavior, learning, thinking, health, appearance, abilities, perceptions, and gender.
>
> (Jennings, 2021, pp. 12–13)

Despite these challenges, many music teachers and education majors continue to persevere and even thrive. While they certainly would not choose to study and teach during a viral pandemic, and would embrace better support for the profession of music teaching, these individuals are able to recognize silver linings and embody hope for the future. "The COVID-19 pandemic has offered us an opportunity to pause, reflect, and take stock of attitudes, beliefs, behavior, and routines" (Wood, 2021, p. 64).

After several decades of studying learned helplessness and other mental deficiencies, Seligman (2018) recognized the need to consider what makes healthy humans function reliably well. Instead of considering mental health exclusively as an absence of maladies, he and other colleagues began suggesting that related research should focus on the additive qualities of positive emotion, engagement, relationships, life meaning, and personal accomplishments (e.g., Carr, 2020; Seligman, 2018).

> I found that merely getting rid of the bad stuff was not enough, and so I advocated working on what makes life worth living as well. Positive psychology complements, but does not displace, working to rid the world of what cripples life.
>
> (Seligman, 2018, p. 276)

In a similar vein, I recently completed a survey of music majors (Bernhard, 2022) in which I compared perceived levels of happiness and gratitude during the second year of the COVID-19 pandemic as compared to three years earlier, before we knew anything about the oncoming virus and related challenges. While average scores were slightly lower overall, standard deviations, or spread of scores, ranged much more widely than before. Some music majors were indeed struggling to find reason for thanksgiving and had very low levels of personal meaning, school engagement, or general enjoyment of life. But others were thriving, even more than in the past. Seniors, in particular, seemed enormously grateful for extra efforts to help them complete field teachings virtually, perform recitals through digital means, and otherwise complete degree requirements that initially seemed unattainable and destined to be delayed. Some found renewed hope and zest for life, recognizing silver linings and opportunities in the unexpected new normal.

This book serves as a sequel to *Managing Stress in Music Education: Routes to Wellness and Vitality* (Bernhard, 2021), in which I suggested that before formal elements of positive psychology can be fully embraced, careful adjustments to personal sleep, physical movement, and nutrition must be negotiated (e.g., Rath, 2013; Wachob, 2016). Sound sleep is one of the most important practices for healthy biological and psychological functioning (e.g., Walker, 2018). Humans need seven to nine hours of uninterrupted rest per night, preferably in a cool and dark environment. Avoiding caffeine, nicotine, and alcohol will help, as will eating small meals throughout the day; getting sufficient daylight exposure, even during the winter; and maintaining enough physical movement. Naps are okay on occasion but should be limited to 30 minutes or less, allowing for proper balance of deep sleep and rapid eye movement dream states during the night. Walker (2018) encouraged us to think of sleep as a free psychological and physical form of therapy. He and his colleagues have completed convincing studies outlining the benefits of sleep to protect against common illnesses such as seasonal colds, as well as deeper psychological setbacks such as anxiety and depression.

Regular physical movement also helps protect against a host of problems and aids tremendously in short-term energy and positive emotion (e.g., Ratey, 2008; Wachob, 2016). While some may consider exercise to be a form of drudgery requiring full marathon training, macho weight lifting, or expensive gym memberships, physical movement should be fun and should include a moderate combination of aerobic activity, strength building, balance, and flexibility (Ratey, 2008). Aerobic activity can include brisk walking, light jogging, tennis, or even lawn mowing and snow blowing. Strive to get 7,000–10,000 steps per day, but don't stress about making it difficult. A few walks around the block in addition to the regular movement of a music education major or teacher should get the job done. Similarly, strength training should be completed in moderation, favoring multiple repetitions with lighter weights over one gigantic "dead lift." Care should be paid to protecting delicate muscles and tendons used for music making. Flexibility and balance are also important, particularly as we age, but even traditional undergraduate music majors reported increased life satisfaction and contentment after a session of yoga or tai chi (e.g., Barbezat & Bush, 2014).

Nutrition is the final piece of a traditional healthy life and, like sleep or physical movement, is described with more detail and application for music educators in *Managing Stress in Music Education*. Practicing sound nutrition helps prevent heart attacks, diabetes, and cancer and aids in prevention of stroke, osteoporosis, constipation, cataracts, and age-related memory loss (e.g., Willett & Skerrett, 2017). Strive for a balance of micro- and macronutrients, limiting salt, sugar, alcohol, and caffeine. Carbohydrates, proteins, and even some healthy fats are important. Seek natural, dark-colored fruits, vegetables, and whole grains. Shopping the perimeters of a traditional grocery store will help you avoid the temptation of processed foods that typically line the shelves of many interior aisles. Eat early in the day, and consider several small meals and snacks, with plenty of water and other hydrating foods and drink (Willett & Skerrett, 2017).

The second half of *Managing Stress in Music Education* served as an introduction to the field of positive psychology, including chapters about gratitude, mindfulness, and "happiness." Gratitude is an essential part of any human life and can be particularly important during times of stress and uncertainty (e.g., Bass, 2018; Emmons, 2007). During the COVID-19 pandemic, music education majors and teachers have sustained and continue to battle many challenges. It is easy to become disheartened and frustrated within such limitations. But recognizing all that is going well, even if not immediately obvious, is necessary for human health and life flourishing. A few years ago, a holiday video made its rounds on social media, in which a father prepared wrapping paper around traditional household items such as light switches, hot water handles, ovens, and a dishwasher. While his wife and children were not initially amused on Christmas morning, they did eventually get the point that humans often fail to recognize the gifts and privileges currently in place until they are taken away. Starting or ending each day with a short list of items for which we are grateful can go a long way toward putting troubles in perspective and recognizing the good in life (Bass, 2018).

Mindfulness is a secular application of ideas from ancient Buddhist practice. Formal mindfulness includes practices like breathing and body scan meditation. While some consider meditation something that would take years to successfully cultivate, breathing meditation can start with as little as 30 seconds to a minute of focus on the breath without judgement or thinking about other worries. Body scan meditation similarly begins with focus on breathing but then moves to awareness and focus on different parts of the body, without judgement, thought, or emotion (e.g., Barbezat & Bush, 2014; Srinivasan, 2014). Formal meditation builds skills for informal mindfulness, which simply involves full awareness of the present moment, again without immediate judgement or emotion. Informal mindfulness can be particularly useful to music educators in the midst of rehearsals or other classes, responding to student behavior challenges, or preparing and presenting formal concerts or recitals. Original practices from Buddhism also include loving-kindness meditation (offering well-wishes to all others) and "Tonglen," a practice of breathing in pain or suffering from others and releasing positive, healing energy while breathing out. Some practitioners also suggest "leaning in" to personal pain or uncertainty, simply being aware of feelings before judging or forming plans for action – responding with equanimity instead of reacting with sudden alarm or panic (e.g., Hawkins, 2017; Srinivasan, 2014).

The chapter in *Managing Stress in Music Education* about "happiness" presented concepts and suggestions related to psychological engagement, life meaning, and positive emotion, but "happiness" can be a confusing term, and the field of positive psychology has continued to expand and develop, particularly during the COVID-19 pandemic (e.g., Carr, 2020; Grenville-Cleave et al., 2021; Wood, 2021). The purpose of this book is to present more detailed and updated research, theory, and best practices related to positive emotion, engagement, relationships, meaning, accomplishment, resilience, and hope. While serious challenges should be addressed by professional medical providers, and attention to systemic changes in education is still needed (e.g., Jennings, 2021), considering these seven variables as routes to general health can help create mental, emotional, and physical pathways to personal and professional flourishing. Although grounded in research, the writing style and the concise nature of coverage are intended to be digestible by busy music educators and college students. Vignettes of hypothetical yet typical music educators will further help set a framework for both pre-service and in-service readers.

Early in the pandemic, I read a social media post from a middle school principal who suggested that teachers would need to afford their students "space and grace" while entering the new period of uncertainty. I suggest that administrators, colleagues, and politicians must also treat teachers in this way and, even more importantly, that we must afford ourselves this same space and grace. By embracing lessons from positive psychology, music education majors and teachers can recognize the good in life; develop autonomy, self-efficacy, and internal locus of control; and position themselves to healthily negotiate the challenges and rewards yet to come.

Summary

- Teaching can be a stressful occupation, particularly during the COVID-19 pandemic.
- Music teachers, in particular, are susceptible to stress and burnout.
- Life stressors beyond music teaching add layers of further challenge.
- The field of positive psychology offers opportunity for relief.
- Consult medical professionals and consider therapeutic interventions.
- Continue efforts for systemic change in the profession.
- Embrace positive emotion, engagement, relationships, meaning, and accomplishment.
- Embrace resilience and hope.

References

Barbezat, D. P., & Bush, M. (2014). *Contemplative practices in higher education: Powerful methods to transform teaching and learning*. Jossey-Bass.

Bass, D. B. (2018). *Grateful: The transformative power of giving thanks*. Harper One.

Bernhard, H. C. (2005). Burnout and the college music education major. *Journal of Music Teacher Education, 15*(1), 43–51.

Bernhard, H. C. (2016). Investigating burnout among elementary and secondary school music educators: A replication. *Contributions to Music Education, 41*, 145–156.

Bernhard, H. C. (2021). *Managing stress in music education: Routes to wellness and vitality*. Routledge.

Bernhard, H. C. (2022). Investigating happiness and gratitude among university music majors during a global pandemic. *Contributions to Music Education, 47*, 175–189.

Carr, A. (2020). *Positive psychology and you: A self-development guide*. Routledge.
Conway, C. M., Micheel-Mays, L., & Micheel-Mays, C. (2005). A narrative study of student teaching and the first year of teaching: Common issues and struggles. *Bulletin of the Council for Research in Music Education, 165*, 65–77.
Emmons, R. A. (2007). *Thanks! How practicing gratitude can make you happier*. Houghton Mifflin Harcourt Publications.
Gilbert, D. (2021). A comparison of self-reported anxiety and depression among undergraduate music majors and nonmusic majors. *Journal of Music Teacher Education, 30*(3), 69–83.
Grenville-Cleave, B., Guomundsdottir, D., Huppert, F., King, V., Roffey, D., Roffey, S., & de Vries, M. (2021). *Creating the world we want to live in: How positive psychology can build a brighter future*. Routledge.
Hamann, D. L. (1986). Burnout and the public school orchestra director. *Update: Applications of Research in Music Education, 4*(3), 11–14.
Hawkins, K. (2017). *Mindful teacher, mindful school: Improving wellbeing in teaching and learning*. Sage.
Jennings, P. A. (2021). *Teacher burnout turnaround: Strategies for empowered educators*. Norton.
Maslach, C., Jackson, S. E., & Leiter, M. P. (1983). *Maslach burnout inventory – manual*. College of California Consulting Psychologists Press.
Mikszka, P., Parkes, K., Russell, J. A., & Bauer, W. (2021). The well-being of music educators during the pandemic: Spring of 2020. *Psychology of Music*, 1–17.
Nápoles, J. (2022). Burnout: A review of the literature. *Update: Applications of Research in Music Education, 40*(2), 19–26.
Parkes, K. A., Russell, J. A., Bauer, W. I., & Miksza, P. (2021). The well-being and instructional experiences of K-12 music educators: Starting a new school year during a pandemic. *Frontiers in Psychology*, 2837.
Perna, M. C. (2022). *Why education is about to reach a crisis of epic proportions*. Retrieved January 8, 2022, from www.forbes.com/sites/markcperna/2022/01/04/why-education-is-about-to-reach-a-crisis-of-epic-proportions/?sh=5d90766978c7
Ratey, J. J. (2008). *Spark: The revolutionary new science of exercise and the brain*. Little, Brown Spark.
Rath, T. (2013). *Eat, move, sleep: How small choices lead to big changes*. Missionday.
Roseth, N. E. (2019). Features of university environments that support well-being as perceived by lesbian, gay, bisexual, and questioning undergraduate music and art students. *Journal of Research in Music Education, 67*(2), 171–192.
Seligman, M. E. P. (2018). *The hope circuit: A psychologist's journey from helplessness to optimism*. Public Affairs.
Srinivasan, M. (2014). *Teach, breathe, learn: Mindfulness in and out of the classroom*. Parallax Press.
Wachob, J. (2016). *Wellth: How to build a life, not a resume*. Harmony Books.
Walker, M. (2018). *Why we sleep: Unlocking the power of sleep and dreams*. Scribner.
Willett, W., & Skerrett, P. (2017). *Eat, drink and be healthy: The Harvard medical school guide to healthy eating*. Simon & Schuster.
Wood, G. W. (2021). *The psychology of wellbeing*. Routledge.

2 Positive Emotion

Olivia is jacked! She's flying down another double black diamond mountain course as part of her university ski team, far ahead of the competition, as usual. Olivia is only a freshman, but she has already eclipsed most team records and loves the thrill of victory. She doesn't bother with training or conditioning much, since she's been skiing as long as she can remember and seems to have a natural ability for blazing speed. During warmer months, she replaces this adrenaline rush with top performances in cross-country running. She was an all-state champion in high school and is expected to improve five-kilometer personal best finishes throughout the remainder of her college career. As with skiing, Olivia isn't interested much in cross-country training, simply loving the rush of putting the pedal to the metal and crushing any competition. Olivia also loves to party and has been drinking, experimenting with drugs, and enjoying multiple sex partners since her junior year of high school. Her favorite college activity so far, even better than top athletic performance, is binging at day-drinking parties until she can no longer see straight.

In addition to these forms of adrenaline rush, Olivia has been accepted to the university's music education major, successfully auditioning on classical saxophone. She much prefers jamming out with high-energy punk rock and heavy metal bands but reluctantly accepts the fact that she must participate in the school's classical saxophone studio in order to be a music teacher. Olivia has fond memories of her own K–12 music teachers and sometimes remembers that they were the one group of mentors who provided safe and calm spaces amidst her turbulent childhood. But later today, Olivia will be observing a local high school concert band rehearsal, and she is looking forward to checking out all the hot senior boys. And later in the month, Olivia is back to racing hard on the slopes, all without sufficient training, sleep, or nutrition, when she feels an unexpected slip on her right ski, catapulting her directly toward a barrier of emergency netting. The last thing Olivia

DOI: 10.4324/9781003331148-2

remembers is the sounds of her coaches and teammates screaming and the distressing feeling of webbed netting consuming her small, mangled body.

Positive emotion is a deep psychological enjoyment of the current moment and can also be recalled from the past or anticipated for the future (e.g., Bono, 2020; Clear, 2018; Diener & Biswas-Diener, 2008; Seligman, 2018; Wood, 2021). During the early years of the positive psychology movement, researchers often labeled positive emotion simply as "pleasure," connecting to its ancient roots. "The doctrine of hedonism – maximizing pleasure and minimizing pain – was articulated thousands of years ago by Aristuppus (435–366 BCE) who championed immediate sensory gratification" (Peterson et al., 2005, p. 25). These researchers developed a survey in which pleasure, meaning, and engagement were measured. While suggesting that some pleasure was psychologically necessary, they emphasized that life meaning (see Chapter 5) and psychological engagement (see Chapter 3) were more important. The researchers found that a healthy distribution among the three variables was approximately 20% pleasure, 40% meaning, and 40% engagement (Peterson et al., 2005).

So while some psychological pleasure is indeed part of human flourishing, too much can cause harm and disease. Consider the opening vignette of Olivia, who finds pleasure in intense athletic competition, relationships with peers and others, and high-energy music making. While in moderation these can be healthy human activities that release endorphins and dopamine, Olivia lets them become obsessions, leading to a problematic overload. In a recent study of university music majors, I found that self-reported levels of pleasure had increased during the COVID-19 pandemic (Bernhard, 2022). "Although extreme emotional highs feel good, they are generally not where the action is in terms of the optimal level of happiness" (Diener & Biswas-Diener, 2008, p. 215). In fact, the resulting disease (or dis-ease) of craving can then become an all-consuming addiction that paralyzes life. "Once a habit has been encoded, the urge to act follows whenever the environmental cues reappear" (Clear, 2018, p. 93).

In music education settings, examples of hedonistic pleasure might include performing a watered-down and simplistic arrangement of other music. While this activity can be immediately enjoyable and perhaps provide some extrinsic motivation for more fulfilling work, the experience on its own will likely result in only brief enjoyment. Deeper levels of interest and engagement will quickly fade, and development of musicianship will be stunted. Similarly, mindlessly watching simple videos, surface-level engagement with social media, and other seemingly fun activities will ultimately lead to distraction. "People who chase continual emotional highs will usually fall short because the biological cards are stacked against their being able to sustain this emotional intensity" (Diener & Biswas-Diener, 2008, p. 216).

Fredrickson (2001) further studied the psychological principle of pleasure and suggested that positive emotion might be a more beneficial relative. She proposed a theory that experiences with positive emotion can not only help in a current moment but can "broaden and build" psychological defense systems to help flourish in later life circumstances. By merely recalling past pleasant events, we can bring increased happiness to current situations. Fredrickson et al. (2000) further found that positive emotion can turn the tide on negative thoughts, which the authors coined the "undoing effect." Thus, in moments of distress, when anxious thoughts cloud our minds, we can find some relief by experiencing or recalling moments of pleasure or positive emotion.

Bono (2020) similarly suggested that recognizing tailwinds in life, as opposed to headwinds, can assist with positive emotion. Consider classroom or rehearsal management, for example, a challenge that causes many music educators to feel frustrated and perhaps even leave the profession. If one recognizes only the times when students misbehave, or the headwinds of the situation, frustration will likely follow, for both teachers and students. Conversely, if teachers can recognize moments when students are on task and contributing positively, or the tailwinds of the situation, positive comments can be offered and students will likely seek further approval. Likewise, recognizing students who are on task, instead of those who are not, can provide an opportunity for them to serve as models or perhaps peer leaders in a given situation.

Bono (2020) also recommended increasing positive emotion by recognizing what we have instead of what we want. He described a related activity in which an equation of division is calculated. If we recognize five items or events that are going well and only one that needs attention, the result is a positive emotion score of five over one, or five total. If we recognize only one item or event that is going well and five that need attention, the result is a positive emotion score of one over five, or only one-fifth (0.20 instead of 5.00). While this might seem a bit simplistic, the human brain is capable of remarkable plasticity in challenging times. Even a brief, purposeful smile or improved posture, sitting up and alert, can provide a quick boost of endorphins and positive emotion (e.g., Brinol et al., 2009).

Bass (2018) suggested that gratitude can be useful for feelings of positive emotion. Personal expressions of gratitude might include strong feelings of appreciation and delight when someone helps or offers a gift of some sort. Communal expressions of gratitude can occur in places of worship, at sporting events, and in music-making environments and have been shown to lessen feelings of loneliness and isolation. According to King and Huppert (2021), "developing a regular practice of appreciating what we are grateful for or what has gone well has been shown to reduce stress, lower blood pressure, boost immunity, and help us sleep better" (p. 10). Leaders from the 2021 Suncoast Music Education Research Symposium supported many of these ideas, including the importance of kindness, mental space, and reflection for positive emotion. Burnard (2021) discussed the importance of mindful silence in order to recognize challenges and opportunities for growth. Fung (2021) posited similar ideas within his philosophical framework of ancient Chinese wisdoms. By recognizing cycles of Yin and Yang, he suggested that the calm and quiet of Yin can be used to prepare for returns of Yang intensity and energy. Kratus (2021) adjusted his well-known concept of "small acts of subversion" to suggest that moments of uncertainty and renewal might also involve small acts of kindness. As music educators and students negotiate post-pandemic challenges and opportunities, gratitude can be a helpful practice to embrace work-life balance and space for reflection.

Recommendations for Healthy Positive Emotion

Enjoy some pleasure, but focus on deeper levels of positive emotion. Carr (2020) outlined several activities for savoring of positive experiences. "Savoring involves deliberately paying attention to, appreciating, enhancing, and prolonging positive experiences and the positive emotions that accompany them" (p. 120). Remembering a meaningful and enjoyable past experience can enhance positive emotion in the present. For example, recalling favorite students from prior years, listening to recordings of outstanding performances from the past, or looking at pictures from trips and other school events from years ago can release endorphins and dopamine in the moment (e.g., Bryant & Veroff, 2007). However, care should be taken to avoid getting mired in the past or to slip into deep nostalgia, which can cause a depressing longing for something far gone (e.g., Seligman, 2018). Carr (2020) also cautioned that care should be practiced to avoid dampening of positive emotion, in which individuals or groups may convince themselves that they are no longer worthy of praise or happiness.

Take a vacation for part of each day, even for a short period of approximately 20 minutes. Listen to an enjoyable recording of music, watch a favorite television show, savor a delicious food or drink, take a mindful walk around the neighborhood, or study a beautiful photograph. These activities can help you live in the present moment and sharpen skills for recognizing and acknowledging positive emotions in other daily settings. While some might describe these activities as self-indulgent or taking too much time, the resulting positive emotion and energy for others will be well worth the small investment. Carr (2020) agreed, adding that "when we act on these, we may change the direction of our lives in ways that will last into the future" (p. 120).

In a similar vein, "hygge" is a Danish term used to convey present-moment awareness of warmth and comfort. The idea was developed in response to cold, harsh, and sometimes boring winters in Nordic regions. Examples of hygge might include gathering with a small group of friends, cuddling with pets, savoring hot beverages, lighting scented candles, or snuggling in a warm blanket. "Hygge (or to be 'hyggeligt') doesn't require learning 'how-to,' adopting it as a lifestyle or buying anything. It literally only requires consciousness, a certain slowness, and the ability to not just be present – but recognize and enjoy the present" (Beauchamp, 2004, p. 1).

Remember healthy levels of sleep, physical movement, and nutrition (e.g., Bernhard, 2021). Having recently completed a long afternoon of snow blowing, I wondered why my machine abruptly stopped working. Thinking that it had overheated and broken, I quickly realized that it was simply out of gasoline. Similarly, music teachers often work on overload without mindfully paying attention to basic needs. Go to bed a little earlier than normal each night, eat something nutritious like a fruit smoothie with a side of oatmeal in the morning, and take an extra walk around the block each day. Small changes will quickly add to big improvements and reframe minor daily annoyances into opportunities for positive emotion. "Habits are the compound interest of self-improvement. . . . they seem to make little difference on any given day and yet the impact they deliver over the months and years can be enormous" (Clear, 2018, p. 16). Physical movement is particularly important, offering opportunities to get outside, improve physical flexibility, and release positive emotion and energizing endorphins (e.g., Ratey, 2008).

Practice gratitude. "Paying attention to what's going well doesn't mean ignoring what's wrong. But it does give us a more constructive and energizing place from which to tackle problems and put things right" (King & Huppert, 2021, p. 11). The research of Pillay et al. (2020) demonstrated that implementing gratitude interventions in small group settings can enable trust and collaboration among participating members. Traditional chamber ensembles or more diverse gatherings of class members can allow opportunities for decision-making regarding existing repertoire or creation of original improvisations and compositions (e.g., Kerchner & Strand, 2016; Randles & Stringham, 2013; Stringham & Bernhard, 2019). Chen et al. (2020) also found that making room for perceived errors or divergent courses of action can be particularly beneficial to creative effort and that gratitude for these possibilities should be embraced.

Shifts in the traditional role of teacher as leader should also be negotiated for increased positive emotion. Arnout and Almoied (2020) noted the importance of both gratitude to others and gratitude from others. Music educators thus have a responsibility of enabling a welcoming and caring classroom or rehearsal environment in which risk-taking is encouraged.

Wang and Cheng (2010) similarly found that students might create most readily as a result of benevolent leadership and autonomy. Autonomy is the notion that individuals who have freedom to self-regulate and responsibility to act alone are more likely to experience life satisfaction than those who are controlled by others. While complete autonomy is neither possible nor beneficial, it is imperative that teachers trust their students and create space for learning while simultaneously receiving latitude and respect from their administration (e.g., King & Huppert, 2021).

Still, there are some moments in music teaching when gratitude or autonomy might not come easily. When teachers feel stifled by political mandates and administrative directives, while students are acting out and disrupting carefully made plans, it's easy to feel very far removed from positive emotion.

> In the chaos and frustrations of the seemingly endless pandemic and societal upheavals, it's so tempting to look for someone or something to blame, the "evil other" who, by virtue of differences in perspective or beliefs, is crafted into a justified target for anger.
>
> (Epstein, 2022, p. 1)

During these challenging moments, practicing curiosity can provide a small space for awareness and healthy response. Why are these mandates in place? Is there room for change? How might I contribute to a new direction? Why is this student misbehaving? Is she frustrated with me? Another student? Something from another class or home life? Remaining curious during times of uncertainty is difficult at best but can cushion pain and gradually lead to opportunities for further positive emotion, such as joy and awe.

Joy and awe are important components of positive emotion and can aid in understanding more comprehensive viewpoints of life. According to Piff et al. (2015), "awe is an emotional response to perceptually vast stimuli that transcend current frames of reference" (p. 883). These researchers analyzed awe and joy across five studies with a collective 2,078 participants and found that the two variables accounted for diminishment of individual concerns and increases in prosocial behavior. In music settings, live concerts and resulting opportunities for audience members to cohabitate physical space can offer prime moments of joy and awe. Even traditional music classrooms and rehearsal halls create space for collective engagement, decreased individual entitlement, and increased group creativity.

Revisiting the music education major, Olivia, from the beginning of this chapter, let's consider how her life would be improved with healthy adjustments to positive emotion. Olivia slowly opens her eyes, recognizing discomfort in her body but still appreciating the beautiful sunrise streaming through the window of her hospital room. She struggles to remember how she ended up here but savors fuzzy memories of many friends and family who have visited with care and love over the past several days. Olivia later learns that she was in a severe ski accident and is lucky to be alive. She will need to recover from several broken bones and bruises, but her relatively young age has spared her further damage, and a full recovery is possible. Instead of rushing things, Olivia and her guardian, who was also Olivia's beginning band teacher, decide that she will take a semester away from college to fully recuperate.

During this time, Olivia slowly regains regular motion in her body, but even more importantly, she focuses on improving her mental health. She enrolls in a mindfulness-based stress reduction course and learns the basics of formal and informal meditation. She also learns yoga, gradually expanding poses and related activities. Olivia cuts back on television, social media, and other smartphone activity, instead opting for reading novels and psychology books. She gradually gets back to saxophone practice, and gratitude for the continued ability changes her perspective from unwanted work to playful enjoyment. While she still enjoys listening to some faster-paced and louder music, she starts to savor the slower and more expansive subtleties of other genres. Olivia focuses on improving her classical saxophone tone quality, her favorite exercises revolving around arrangements of the Bach Cello Suites.

Olivia later reenrolls at the university and soon finds herself back in music education classes and field experiences. While she is still technically a freshman, she is a year older than peers in her cohort. She smiles with amusement at how immature some of her classmates behave. During a high school field experience, other majors fret about how they look and whether the high schoolers will think they're cool. Olivia simply breathes deeply, takes a step back, and notices a young boy struggling with saxophone. She slowly walks over and introduces herself, calmly demonstrating a few tips for success as the band finishes assembling. Olivia notices herself feeling like her own childhood music teachers, warm and encouraging. . . ., but without any sort of friend or peer connection. Olivia returns to campus, confident that she's in the right major, changes into some comfortable workout clothes, and heads out for a slow but steady run around campus. She is happy. She is free.

Summary

- Enjoy some pleasure, but limit to healthy levels.
- Savor positive experiences in the moment.
- Try the Danish art of hygge.

16 *Positive Emotion*

- Broaden and build to recall past positive experiences and future opportunities.
- Enjoy healthy sleep, physical movement, and nutrition.
- Practice gratitude. Notice the tailwinds when challenged by headwinds.
- Encourage autonomy, for yourself and others.
- Slow down to avoid information overload.
- Practice curiosity during moments of uncertainty or frustration.
- Seek opportunities for deep joy and awe.
- Remember why you chose to be a music educator. Recognize the good.

References

Arnout, B. A., & Almoied, A. A. (2020). A structural model relating gratitude, resilience, psychological well-being, and creativity among psychological counsellors. *Counselling and Psychotherapy Research*, 1–20.

Bass, D. B. (2018). *Grateful: The transformative power of giving thanks*. Harper One.

Beauchamp, A. (2004). *Hygge definition and introduction to Hygge House*. Retrieved February 5, 2022, from https://hyggehouse.com/hygge

Bernhard, H. C. (2021). *Managing stress in music education: Routes to wellness and vitality*. Routledge.

Bernhard, H. C. (2022). Investigating happiness and gratitude among university music majors during a global pandemic. *Contributions to Music Education, 47*, 175–189.

Bono, T. (2020). *Happiness 101: Simple secrets to smart living and well-being*. Grand Central.

Brinol, P., Petty, R. E., & Wagner, B. (2009). Body posture effects on self-evaluation: A self- validation approach. *European Journal of Social Psychology, 39*(6), 1053–1064.

Bryant, F. B., & Veroff, J. (2007). *Savouring: A new model of positive experience*. Lawrence Erlbaum.

Burnard, P. (2021, January 27–30). *Conference discussant* [Symposium]. Suncoast Music Education Research Symposium, Tampa, FL.

Carr, A. (2020). *Positive psychology and you: A self-development guide*. Routledge.

Chen, L., Guo, Y., Song, L. J., & Lyu, B. (2020). From errors to OCBs and creativity: A multilevel mediation mechanism of workplace gratitude. *Current Psychology*, 1–15.

Clear, J. (2018). *Atomic habits: An easy and proven way to build good habits and break bad ones*. Avery.

Diener, E., & Biswas-Diener, R. (2008). *Happiness: Unlocking the mysteries of psychological wealth*. Blackwell.

Epstein, R. (2022). *Furious to curious*. Retrieved February 6, 2022, from https://mindfulpracticeinmedicine.com/furious-to-curious/

Fredrickson, B. L. (2001). The role of positive emotions in positive psychology: The broaden- and-build theory of positive emotions. *American Psychologist*, *56*, 218–226.
Fredrickson, B. L., Mancuso, R. A., Branigan, C., & Tugade, M. M. (2000). The undoing effect of positive emotions. *Motivation and Emotion*, *24*, 237–258.
Fung, V. (2021, January 27–30). *Conference discussant* [Symposium]. Suncoast Music Education Research Symposium, Tampa, FL.
Kerchner, J. L., & Strand, K. (Eds.). (2016). *Musicianship: Composing in choir*. GIA Publishing.
King, V., & Huppert, F. (2021). Foundations for a brighter future. In B. Grenville-Cleave, D. Guomundsdottir, F. Huppert, V. King, D. Roffey, S. Roffey, & M. de Vries (Eds.), *Creating the world we want to live in: How positive psychology can build a brighter future* (pp. 3–19). Routledge.
Kratus, J. (2021, January 27–30). *Conference discussant* [Symposium]. Suncoast Music Education Research Symposium, Tampa, FL.
Peterson, C., Park, N., & Seligman, M. E. P. (2005). Orientation to happiness and life satisfaction: The full life versus the empty life. *Journal of Happiness Studies*, *6*, 25–41.
Piff, P. K., Dietze, P., Feinberg, M., Stancato, D. M., & Keltner, D. (2015). Awe, the small self, and prosocial behavior. *Journal of Personality and Social Psychology*, *108*(6), 883–899.
Pillay, N., Park, G., Kim, Y. K., & Lee, S. (2020). Thanks for your ideas: Gratitude and team creativity. *Organizational Behavior and Human Decision Processes*, *156*, 69–81.
Randles, C., & Stringham, D. A. (Eds.). (2013). *Musicianship: Composing in band and orchestra*. GIA Publishing.
Ratey, J. J. (2008). *Spark: The revolutionary new science of exercise and the brain*. Little, Brown Spark.
Seligman, M. E. P. (2018). *The hope circuit: A psychologist's journey from helplessness to optimism*. Public Affairs.
Stringham, D. A., & Bernhard, H. C. (Eds.). (2019). *Musicianship: Improvising in band and orchestra*. GIA Publishing.
Wang, A. C., & Cheng, B. S. (2010). When does benevolent leadership lead to creativity? The moderating role of creative role identity and job autonomy. *Journal of Organizational Behavior*, *31*(1), 106–121.
Wood, G. W. (2021). *The psychology of wellbeing*. Routledge.

3 Engagement

Nathaniel drums his fingers anxiously, trying to figure out what to do with his 27-minute planning period. Other teachers receive twice the time for planning each day, but because Nathaniel is a "specials" teacher, he is expected to monitor seventh graders in the cafeteria during Period 5B. Nathaniel starts to write an overdue lesson plan, but the task leads him to fret about his upcoming teaching observation. He checks his email to see if the principal has clarified expectations for that observation but gets distracted by a message from an angry parent. Frustrated after reading the parent's comments, Nathaniel abruptly closes his email, posts a rant on Twitter,

DOI: 10.4324/9781003331148-3

and spends the remainder of his planning period playing an online game of Mortal Kombat. Hurrying down the hall and resenting his upcoming cafeteria duty, Nathaniel fails to notice the beautiful weather outside or the lovely student artwork recently displayed around the school. Nathaniel's sour mood spills into the cafeteria, where he yells at several students who are innocently laughing and having a good time. The students roll their eyes at Nathaniel, wondering why he's so moody and stating their overall disdain for his music classes.

The students might respect Nathaniel better if he could focus the curriculum of his general music classes. As an aspiring opera singer in college, Nathaniel didn't pay much attention to general music methods, so he started the year by projecting videos of full opera performances for his students to watch. They laugh at what they deem to be ridiculous old costumes and wigs, yodel with humorous imitations of what they think opera singers sound like, and express frustration and boredom at the length of these "crazy" productions. Nathaniel reacts angrily and abruptly shifts focus several times each month. "Fine, if you don't like that music, I'll play you other YouTube videos. Anything to keep you quiet!" The students continue to be irritated, disinterested by the lack of engagement or musical challenge. Nathaniel ends up requiring every student to write a final class paper about why they can't behave properly.

Psychological engagement is the ability to focus on a task at hand or a series of life goals without disruption. When experienced in its purest form, a feeling of euphoria or deep life satisfaction can be attained (e.g., Carr, 2020; Qualman, 2020; Wood, 2021). Csikszentmihalyi (1991) coined the term "flow," in which individuals or communal groups become deeply engaged in an activity to the point that clock time seems to pass without effort. "The defining feature of flow is total experiential adsorption in an activity and temporary loss of awareness of other aspects of the self and one's life situation" (Carr, 2020, p. 135). For an activity to induce flow, it must be neither too difficult nor too easy. In a music setting, students are sometimes bored by the ease of literature or simply uninterested in a topic, such as the case with Nathaniel's classes that don't understand classical opera. Similarly, students can be overwhelmed by too much challenge, perhaps lacking prerequisite skills and knowledge and thus giving up in frustration.

For psychological flow and engagement to occur naturally, an activity must not be too easy or difficult but should provide sufficient challenge to have interest and merit of study. Music students will need a variety of engaging problems to solve, with gradual increases of intensity. For groups of heterogeneous background, peer teaching and learning can be an effective strategy (e.g., Webb, 2015). Challenge more experienced students to share their abilities with those who are less experienced. While care should be taken to monitor social implications, such arrangements can lessen teacher burden and encourage class autonomy for both groups of students. A friend of mine was teaching a 9th–12th grade orchestra that included both a freshman violinist who struggled with the concept of sharps versus naturals (not to mention the executive skills to play those differences in tune) and a senior exchange student who was a substitute cellist with the local professional orchestra. What a difference in ability levels! While rehearsals were initially challenging, and beyond boring for the senior, the teacher gradually incorporated chamber ensembles into her curriculum and invited the cellist and other advanced students to guide their peers. There were still moments of difficulty and unrest, but for the most part, all students appreciated the opportunity to be more independent, and even those who initially lacked experience rose to the challenge of learning from their peers.

Unfortunately, the human ability to concentrate enough for psychological engagement seems to be deteriorating, leading to scattered feelings of nervousness and anxiety.

> In the year 2000, the average adolescent attention span was twelve seconds. . . . today, the average attention span has dropped to eight seconds and the culprit seems to be social media and the Internet. One study reported that young adults between the ages of eighteen and thirty-three interact with their phones an astounding eighty-five times a day, spending several hours doing so.
>
> (Elmore & McPeak, 2019, p. 49)

Similarly, Carr (2008) argued that, while the current culture of simply Googling answers in both scholarship and pop culture can be useful, it is likely leading to difficulties engaging with full-text books and articles. "The way we live is eroding our capacity for deep, sustained, perceptive attention – the building block of intimacy, wisdom, and cultural progress" (Jackson, 2009, p. 13).

The challenge of distraction seems to only be worsening during the COVID-19 pandemic, as the makers and marketers of news purposely present negative stories and misleading headlines, sometimes referred to as "click bait," to lure consumers deeper and deeper down a rabbit hole of digital distraction. Music educators may struggle with these temptations due to the uncertainty of future plans. Will traditional concerts and festivals return? Can ensembles rehearse in former seating arrangements? Are school-sponsored day travels and longer field trips permitted amidst virus concerns? And it's also important to recognize that students may struggle with distraction while returning to schools. When home life has been disrupted by learning loss, economic struggle, and social disfunction, teachers become responsible for helping refocus an anxious population of young minds.

Miksza et al. (2021) surveyed 2,023 PK–12 and collegiate music teachers at the beginning of the COVID-19 pandemic and found that participants reported significantly lower levels of psychological engagement than published norms. I found similar results when surveying music education majors (Bernhard, 2020, 2022). While scores for meaning and gratitude were quite strong, scores for engagement were surprisingly low, particularly once the pandemic arrived. "It drains our energy and attitude. It negatively impacts our health, our work, our well-being, and our families. . . . The disease? Our inability to focus on what matters most" (Qualman, 2020, p. 3).

Patience is often needed for deep levels of psychological engagement. In contrast to surface levels of involvement, taking time to slow the pace of life and even embrace occasional boredom can help people experience meaningful levels of flow.

> Much in the way that athletes must take care of their bodies outside of their training sessions, you'll struggle to achieve the deepest levels of concentration if you spend the rest of your time fleeing the slightest hint of boredom.
>
> (Newport, 2016, p. 157)

In a classic experiment from the 1960s, researchers at Stanford University presented young children with a marshmallow, inviting them to eat it but offering a second option in which the children would receive two marshmallows if they could resist the temptation of eating the first one for a few minutes. In later life, participants who were able to display patience were more likely to be successful academically and socially than their peers who immediately consumed the first marshmallow (Duhigg, 2014).

After patience has been exercised, resulting in improved psychological engagement, savoring of pleasant experiences can and should be employed (see Chapter 2 for further details). "Savoring involves deliberately paying attention to, appreciating, enhancing and prolonging positive experiences and the positive emotions that accompany them, and preventing the rapid adaptation to positive experiences associated with the hedonic treadmill" (Carr, 2020, p. 141). Most music educators have at least a small collection of fond memories, whether they be powerful recollections of undergraduate studies and music major friends or uplifting teaching moments and positive interactions with students. While reminiscing about these experiences can be psychologically beneficial, it is even better to notice and savor them in the moment. Recognizing these positive reasons for enjoying music education and deepening the pleasure in the moment can greatly offset challenging moments and can remind music educators why they enjoy their profession and why hope for the future is likely.

Savoring and engagement can also aid in the process of creativity. Csikszentmihalyi (2013) extended his theory of psychological flow to suggest that discovery and invention can be enhanced when focus is honed. Wang and Cheng (2010) studied connections between leadership style and creativity of workers via 167 dyads of supervisors and subordinates in Taiwanese technology companies. The researchers found that benevolent leaders positively impacted the creativity of those they guided and that the connection was particularly strong when subordinates perceived autonomy and strong role identity in their work. In a music setting, this might translate to a more welcoming space for students to influence their own learning environment. Identifying a rotation of student leaders for the day or week, or shifting to chamber groups in lieu of conductor-led large ensembles, can increase student autonomy and thus promote greater focus and psychological engagement during music-making activities.

Burnard's (2012) work regarding musical creativities resonates with many of these research findings. She posited a multidimensional model of creativities in which individuals rely on one another and sometimes change roles within a complex web of music, technology, industries, commerce, cultural production, and social spaces. "Musicians are constantly repositioning themselves across multiple fields. From the collective creativity of collaborative teams to the empathic creativity of improvised musics, we see musicians broaden their remit and locate their work across different industries" (p. 217). Within such a complex system, awareness of relationships and gratitude for resulting symbiosis and psychological engagement can aid in furthering creativities.

Recommendations for Healthy Psychological Engagement

Newport (2016) argued that many adults and children purposely seek distraction as a psychological excuse to avoid deep focus. This can translate to spending excessive time and energy answering emails, checking text messages, scheduling and attending unnecessary meetings, and chatting superficially with others. "This type of work is inevitable, but you must keep it confined to a point where it doesn't impede your ability to take full advantage of the deeper efforts that ultimately determine your impact" (p. 221). Setting timers for both deep work and potential distractors can help manage time. Digital apps are available to purposefully block access to social media platforms and other online temptations.

Related sounds and images pull at our attention and cause unhealthy levels of dependency and distraction. While social media can be useful in certain settings, the proliferation of platforms and ease of sharing can cause an overwhelming sense of information overload. "Willpower is limited, and therefore the more enticing tools you have pulling at your attention, the harder it'll be to maintain focus on something important" (Newport, 2016, p. 182). To counteract these challenges, reduce screen time and choose only one or two platforms for activity. If regularly sharing on social media sites, reduce activity gradually, posting only once per day, then once every other day, then once per week, etc. Carefully consider whether every idea or experience is worthy of sharing, and remember how many different people, from different facets of your life, will be viewing the resulting content.

Email and text messaging can be similar drains on psychological engagement. Experiment with notification settings on smartphones and tablets, choosing selected times of day to check messages and otherwise ignoring the devices. Maintain separate accounts for work and home, limiting professional interactions to school hours. If it becomes convenient to write email messages beyond regular work hours, auto-schedule the sending of those messages such that immediate responses cannot be received during personal time. Newport (2016) suggested the possibility of a full exit from Internet consumption, and if that is not feasible, a "sabbatical" or "sabbath." "The latter asks that you regularly take small breaks (usually a single weekend day), while the former describes a substantial and long break from an online life, lasting many weeks – and sometimes more" (p. 183).

Make a list and prioritize what is most important, personally and professionally. Qualman (2020) suggested making a "not-to-do list," helping identify menial tasks and disruptions that deter psychological engagement. Music educators often overschedule and work too superficially on many projects instead of deeply on a few. This practice can also spill into personal life, with overloaded schedules and surface-level participation in a myriad of activities. Instead, brainstorm to isolate three areas that are most important for your career and personal life. What do you value most? For example, such consideration might lead to more enjoyment of one leisure activity and help you determine a curricular focus for the coming year or two. While quiet time alone is a good place to start, working with a trusted friend, colleague, or administrator can help you healthily process ideas. "An accountability partner can create an immediate cost to inaction. We care deeply about what others think of us" (Clear, 2018, p. 211).

Know when to say no. Music educators are often people-pleasers, wanting to advocate for their area by accepting extra responsibilities and spreading themselves too thin. While this type of activity can look impressive on a surface level, constant busyness saps energy and leads to lower levels of performance than possible when deeply engaged. While feelings of guilt may result, politely declining some requests, particularly those that do not align with your signature strengths (see Chapter 5), will create space for improved teaching, learning, and musicianship. "Be selfish. It's your schedule, not theirs. There's no way to reach your goals if you're taking on everyone else's challenges and forgetting about your own" (Qualman, 2020, p. 84).

Like many other components of positive psychology, mindfulness practice can aid in focus. Smookler (2022) wrote that related formal and informal activities can help people stay present when there is temptation to panic.

> Mindfulness can invite us to notice what we need to be well. Then when life drops us onto roller coasters, we can maintain our seat. We can make space for what we need, while also offering ourselves myriad ways to stay open and present to the grand adventure of every moment.
> (p. 27)

A particularly useful form of mindfulness practice for music teachers involves that of listening. As we interact with the psychological properties of pitch, rhythm, timbre, and loudness and rehearse for intonation, tone quality, articulation, precision, phrasing, balance, and blend, it is imperative that we sharpen listening acuity. Mindfulness practices offer an opportunity to deepen listening skills for both music and spoken language. According to Barbezat and Bush (2014), "deep listening is a way of hearing in which we are fully present with what is happening in the moment. . . . very few have developed this capacity for listening" (p. 137). In rehearsal settings and classes, students could be encouraged to listen specifically for bass lines, melodies, or harmonies; close their eyes to listen for those singing or playing the same part; or simply attend to silence occurring within a given musical excerpt. These exercises can be extended to other aspects of life, listening for weather patterns while walking outside, listening for mechanical sounds while inside, and listening with focused purpose while engaged in conversation with others (Hawkins, 2017; Jennings, 2015; Srinivasan, 2014).

Prioritizing tasks that need to happen sooner rather than later allows space to successfully complete expectations on time, pushing more pleasurable activities or things that can wait until later in the day (sometimes being bumped to a later date if needed). Tracy (2002) presented the concept of "eating that frog," translating to completing essential tasks for a given day as early as possible. "The purpose of time-management skills, of eating that frog, and getting more done in less time, is to enable you to spend more face time with the people you care about, doing the things that give you the greatest amount of joy in life" (p. 1).

For music education majors, these suggestions might translate to scheduling 90 minutes of individual focus each day. The first 30 minutes might be dedicated to a careful warm-up practice session, the second 30 minutes to mindful exercise, and the final 30 minutes to study or work on a long-term class project. Thus, gradual progress is made in each area, decreasing the anxiety of procrastination and increasing psychological flow. Music teachers could go to sleep one hour earlier than usual and use the extra 60 minutes each morning to exercise, meditate, and plan for the new day. Instead of scurrying into school each morning, the new plan allows for calm and centered space in which challenges can be addressed and positive moments can be fully embraced.

Similarly, scheduling breaks throughout a given day provides space for relaxation and contemplation. Current society, particularly related to the music education profession, is often obsessed with busyness and productivity. While these can seem like worthy goals, constant activity, in addition to perceptions of others being one step ahead of us, usually leads to feelings of anxiety and fatigue. Creating time to simply be will often help reduce stress and ultimately enhance productivity.

> The people who maintain a happy life, those who are emotionally healthy, are people who create margin in their calendars. They schedule portions of their days to create space. They remove noise and clutter during those portions of time. They experience solitude. Quiet. Simplicity. They take control of their days instead of remaining at the mercy of all the busyness going on. They are intentional to unplug.
> (Elmore & McPeak, 2019, p. 146).

Using suggestions from this chapter, let's now revisit the general music teacher, Nathaniel, from a more engaged and focused perspective. Nathaniel enrolls in an eight-week mindfulness-based stress reduction course and learns the basics of meditation. While he still doesn't find much time for formal mindfulness, he has started a morning routine of waking 30 minutes earlier than before and embracing informal mindfulness while savoring hot coffee and gradually preparing for his day. He laughs warmly with one of his students during his 27-minute planning period. The two of them are reviewing guitar chords, and the student is sharing a short tune he created the previous night. Another student is excitedly working across the room, mixing loops at a school computer station. Nathaniel calls out across the room, "Hey, Brad, give us a bass line!" Brad shares a simple four-measure loop, and the guitar student, stumbling playfully at first, creates interesting improvisations to match.

The two students and Nathaniel can't believe how quickly the 27 minutes have passed but agree to keep chatting about future possibilities as they head to the cafeteria. The student who was at the computer notices an impressive array of cloud formations out the window and notes that it would be cool to create some digital tracks in that mood. The guitarist agrees and realizes that they could ask other students to add accompanying artwork. "There's so much talent at this school; just look at these wall displays!" The energy among these three is infectious to the point that other students start huddling around their continued conversations in the cafeteria. Within the next few weeks, positive momentum has led to music "informances" during lunch periods, creating more excitement and the start of an extracurricular rock band. Nathaniel's popularity and respect grow to a point that students even want to know more about his experience with opera. "What was that weird stuff you were showing us on YouTube?" Instead of sharing more videos, Nathaniel invites some of his peers from his undergraduate years to join his classes in conversations and demonstrations of opera, including some modern adaptations. While not every student is initially hooked, they're willing to engage and start experimentations toward a rock opera that will be created and produced by general music classes later in the year.

Summary

- Be aware of the present moment. Savor the good.
- Encourage focus and autonomy for increased creativity.
- Limit screen time.
- Limit email and social media.
- Take extra time for rest, working more deeply less often.
- Embrace boredom to avoid distraction.
- Perform mundane tasks with mindfulness.
- Perform complex tasks in stages.
- Use timers and small rewards for motivation.
- Make a list and prioritize what is most important, personally and professionally.
- Learn to say no.
- Be patient, with yourself and others.

References

Barbezat, D. P., & Bush, M. (2014). *Contemplative practices in higher education: Powerful methods to transform teaching and learning.* Jossey-Bass.

Bernhard, H. C. (2020). An investigation of happiness and gratitude among music majors. *New Directions in Music Education, 4,* 1–10.

Bernhard, H. C. (2022). Investigating happiness and gratitude among university music majors during a global pandemic. *Contributions to Music Education, 47,* 175–189.

Burnard, P. (2012). *Musical creativities in practice*. Oxford.
Carr, A. (2020). *Positive psychology and you: A self-development guide*. Routledge.
Carr, N. (2008, July/August). Is googling making us stupid? *The Atlantic*.
Clear, J. (2018). *Atomic habits: An easy and proven way to build good habits and break bad ones*. Avery.
Csikszentmihalyi, M. (1991). *Flow: The psychology of optimal experience*. Harper Perennial Modern Classics.
Csikszentmihalyi, M. (2013). *Creativity: The psychology of discovery and invention*. Harper Perennial Modern Classics.
Duhigg, C. (2014). *The power of habit: Why we do what we do in life and in business*. Random House.
Elmore, T., & McPeak, A. (2019). *Generation Z unfiltered: Facing nine hidden challenges of the most anxious population*. Poet Gardener.
Hawkins, K. (2017). *Mindful teacher, mindful school: Improving wellbeing in teaching and learning*. Sage.
Jackson, M. (2009). *Distracted: The erosion of attention and the coming dark age*. Prometheus Books.
Jennings, P. A. (2015). *Mindfulness for teachers: Simple skills for peace and productivity in the classroom*. W. W. Norton.
Miksza, P., Parkes, K., Russell, J. A., & Bauer, W. (2021). The well-being of music educators during the pandemic: Spring of 2020. *Psychology of Music*, 1–17.
Newport, C. (2016). *Deep work: Rules for focused success in a distracted world*. Piatkus.
Qualman, E. (2020). *The focus project: How to focus in an unfocused world*. Equalman Studios.
Smookler, E. (2022). Finding a way to keep your seat. *Mindful Magazine*, *9*(6), 26–27.
Srinivasan, M. (2014). *Teach, breathe, learn: Mindfulness in and out of the classroom*. Parallax Press.
Tracy, B. (2002). *Eat that frog: 21 great ways to stop procrastinating and get more done in less time*. Berrett-Koehler.
Wang, A. C., & Cheng, B. S. (2010). When does benevolent leadership lead to creativity? The moderating role of creative role identity and job autonomy. *Journal of Organizational Behavior*, *31*(1), 106–121.
Webb, R. S. (2015). An exploration of three peer tutoring cases in the school orchestra program. *Bulletin of the Council for Research in Music Education*, *203*, 63–80.
Wood, G. W. (2021). *The psychology of wellbeing*. Routledge.

4 Relationships

Randi looks longingly into the hallway from behind her classroom piano. The bell to end another school day has just sounded, and she's jealous of her high school students who congregate with one another, excitedly preparing for a Friday evening of fun. Randi feels like her own social life peaked in high school and college and can't figure out why she struggles with human connection outside school. Other teachers in the school are a generation older, and since Randi is responsible for choir, general music, and band (there is no string orchestra program at this high school), she has no music colleagues in her building. Randi had been somewhat excited about some new scores she ordered, but instead of reviewing them and writing lesson plans for the following week, she sullenly flips through pages of her own high school yearbook. She wrongly assumes that all her former friends are too busy with their own jobs and personal lives to care what Randi might be doing or to rekindle any sort of relationships.

Randi also struggles to communicate with her building principal, assuming that he is out to get her and that he does not care about her music program. The two of them got off to a rough start this year when Randi refused a bus duty assignment, arguing that she needed early morning time to work with individual students before first period. Yesterday, the principal sent Randi a short email message stating that he needs to see lesson plans from her past three weeks of teaching and would like to observe two of her rehearsals as soon as possible. Randi assumes the worst, that something must be wrong, and thus chooses to ignore the message, letting it sit with thousands of other emails yet to be opened.

Randi exits a side door of the music room, which is located near the back of the building, and walks sluggishly to her car, avoiding any possible contact with her principal. She had registered for a community bowling group that afternoon but hasn't eaten anything all day, so instead she drives mindlessly back to her empty apartment. Randi has a text message from her mother, suggesting a videoconference chat, but Randi instead

DOI: 10.4324/9781003331148-4

Relationships 29

scrolls through social media, envying the posts of others and dropping further into low energy and sadness. Randi's apartment has very little light, with all the window blinds drawn shut. Her cupboards are bare, so she orders a large pizza and a liter of soda and prepares for a solo night of Netflix binging.

Like many music teachers, Randi feels isolated in her school building and spends so much time and energy teaching that she has very little left to negotiate human relationships. Yet relationships are an essential component of healthy living, psychological flourishing, and successful teaching. This has become particularly apparent during the COVID-19 pandemic, as many people have been isolated by living alone, communicating exclusively through digital means, and struggling to interact traditionally with other human beings. "At all levels, from families to organizations, communities, and nations, it is the quality of our relationships with each other, and the positivity in those connections, that make the most difference for wellbeing" (Roffey, 2021, p. 91). Even prior to the pandemic, researchers found that many music majors and teachers felt underappreciated compared to their peers in other subjects (e.g., Gilbert, 2021; Payne et al., 2020) and that in rural or smaller school districts, they might be the only music teacher, or the only one with a particular specialty, within their building (Sindberg & Lipscomb, 2005).

Before connections with other human beings can be successfully negotiated, relationships with oneself must be healthy. Attention and proper adjustments to sleep, physical movement, and nutrition will aid in a solid foundation for mental health. Endorphins from exercise, fuel from food, and alertness from sleep are critical (e.g., Bernhard, 2021; Rath, 2013). For those still struggling with self-esteem and acceptance, working with a certified therapist can help address underlying trauma and other challenges. As stated during traditional airline flights, an oxygen mask should be used for oneself before assisting others; if you are incapacitated, there is no chance of helping elsewhere. "Our sense of self is the primary foundation for relationships with others. It informs what we need in our relationships, and whether we tend to see others as a threat, or an ally" (Roffey, 2021, p. 93).

Bowlby (1988) developed "attachment theory," suggesting that individuals who experienced nurturing and fulfilling childhood interactions with their parents tend to feel more confident and at ease in adult relationships. Individuals who experienced secure parental attachments had basic needs met, such as food, warmth, and protection from general dangers. They also received deeper levels of love and support as children, both physically and emotionally. Individuals with insecure parental attachments might have experienced severe lack of even basic needs but also could have had some needs met while still lacking proper emotional support. According to Carr (2020), these deficiencies manifest in adulthood as avoidant attachment and anxious attachment. Avoidant adult relationships are characterized by lack of trust to the point that individuals resist invitations for closeness, assuming that relationships could lead to problems. Anxious adult relationships are characterized by a clinging need for security. These people are convinced that others will desert them, to the point of mistrust and unhealthy dependency.

Once attention to the self has been achieved, researchers suggest that both deep and casual connections with others are important. While it is not realistic to know all acquaintances at an intimate level, having one or two other human beings who can be deeply trusted and known is important. Spouses, partners, siblings, parents, and good friends can serve as sounding boards for conversation and can provide emotional support in times of challenge and celebration. Bradford and Robin (2021) labeled these types of relationships as "exceptional" and suggested that they have six typical characteristics:

> 1) You can be more fully yourself, and so can the other person. 2) Both of you are willing to be vulnerable. 3) You trust that self-disclosures will not be used against you. 4) You can be honest with each other. 5) You deal with conflict productively. 6) Both of you are committed to each other's growth and development.
>
> (p. 4)

More casual human connection is also important and can include simple greetings with neighbors, store workers, and random others on the street. Even a friendly smile or nod can go a long way in lifting human spirits. Informal professional relationships can provide another layer of human connection. Creating space for weekly check-ins or short visits to colleagues' offices and classrooms can make a positive impact. Opportunities to share challenges and successes can be particularly important for itinerant teachers, who often feel isolated while traveling among different school campuses (e.g., Bernhard, 2016; Hedden, 2005).

In the field of music education, relationships with students are particularly important. While teachers often dream of creating little versions of themselves, awareness and respect for student diversity are essential. Jennings (2021) recommended that we should meet others where they are, instead of trying to mold them into likenesses of ourselves. "To provide high quality emotional support to others, we must be able to see them for who they are, not who we wish they would be or in terms of how they are 'supposed' to be" (p. 54). Roffey (2021) stated that challenges with any relationship, but with students in particular, include criticism, contempt, defensiveness, and stonewalling. Criticism and contempt can occur for both teachers and students and involve feelings of negativity that often lead to verbal or emotional attacks. Defensiveness and stonewalling occur most often with students but can also occur for teachers. Instead of admitting challenges and asking for help, students will often shut down, developing excuses for participation and lack of participation.

Recommendations for Healthy Relationships and Connection

Carr (2020) recommended five key practices for focusing on relationships: compassion and loving-kindness meditation, acts of kindness, volunteering, celebrating success, and understanding attachment styles. Compassion and loving-kindness meditation draws its roots from ancient religious practices such as Buddhism but has also gained widespread acceptance and practice in secular settings. In addition to the following exercise, mindfulness activities and suggestions from chapter 7 of *Managing Stress in Music Education* may be helpful (Bernhard, 2021).

> Sit in a chair with feet flat on the floor, the spine straight and not resting against the chair back, and the eyes gently closed. Adopt an erect, dignified and comfortable posture. Bring awareness to sensations in the lower abdominal wall as the breath moves in and out of the body. Then expand attention to your whole body. When your mind wanders, as it inevitably will, acknowledge where it went. Then bring your attention back to the breath or the body, whichever you were focusing on when the mind wandered.
>
> When you are ready, allow some of these phrases to come to mind: May I be free from suffering, harm, pain, distress, and illness. May I be happy, have well-being, and have joy in my life. May I live with ease, live in peace, and be safe. . . . Allow these phrases to become a doorway through which you can experience a deep sense of compassion, kindness, or friendship towards yourself.
>
> Now visualize someone you love. Wish them well in the same way. Acknowledge that they, like you, have challenges in their lives and want to be happy. . . . May they be free from suffering, harm, pain, distress, and illness. May they be happy, have well-being, and have joy in their life. May they live with ease, live in peace, and be safe.
>
> When you are ready to move on, visualize a stranger. This may be someone you see regularly when shopping or traveling to work. Although you recognize them, you do not know them well, and have

no strong feelings about them, either positive or negative. Wish them well in the same way. Acknowledge that they, like you, have challenges in their lives and want to be happy. . . . May they be free from suffering, harm, pain, distress, and illness. May they be happy, have well-being, and have joy in their life. May they live with ease, live in peace, and be safe.

When you are ready to move on, visualize someone whom you find difficult, someone who you find it hard to experience kindness towards, but not the most difficult person you know. Although you find them difficult and would rather avoid them, acknowledge that they, like you, have challenges in their lives, hopes and dreams, and want to be happy . . . . May they be free from suffering, harm, pain, distress, and illness. May they be happy, have well-being, and have joy in their life. May they live with ease, live in peace, and be safe. . . . If, at any time, you feel overwhelmed by intense feelings or thoughts, direct your attention to the breath to anchor yourself in the present moment, treating yourself with kindness and compassion.

Finally, extend loving kindness to all beings including people you love, strangers, those whom you find difficult, and yourself. . . . May they be free from suffering, harm, pain, distress, and illness. May they be happy, have well-being, and have joy in their life. May they live with ease, live in peace, and be safe.

From time to time, the mind will wander away from the focus of compassion. You may find thoughts, images, plans, or daydreams coming up. This is what the mind naturally does. When this happens, acknowledge it, noticing where the mind has wandered. . . . Then gently return your attention to the focus of your compassion.

At the conclusion of this meditation, direct your attention to the breath in the body, resting in clear awareness of the present moment; accepting whatever feelings may be present without judgement; and taking particular note of whatever feelings of warmth, generosity, and love you may find in your heart.

(Carr, 2020, pp. 205–208)

In a similar vein to compassion and loving-kindness meditation, acts of kindness and volunteering offer opportunities to express care for fellow human beings, thus improving relationships and increasing personal happiness. Acts of kindness might include buying coffee for a colleague, helping a student with a music or personal problem, giving money to a school fundraising project, or filling in for another teacher's lunch duty. While important to protect personal space and time, occasionally performing acts of kindness, especially when done without expectation of reciprocity, can help school environments function more healthily (e.g., Carr, 2020; Jennings, 2021).

Volunteering might best be done outside the school environment to avoid confusion between job responsibilities and extra service. This is particularly important for music teachers, who are often expected to teach among several school buildings and offer instruction beyond normal school hours. Working at homeless shelters, volunteering for literacy workshops, coaching a community sports team, or visiting senior living centers can all provide a change of pace from music teaching and can create a win-win situation in which the community of those serving and those served all benefit (e.g., Roffey, 2021).

Gilbert (2010) outlined a theory for regulating emotions, which helps explain why compassion and loving-kindness meditation, acts of kindness, and volunteering might be beneficial for improved relationships. He stated that there are three primary systems for regulating human emotions, each represented by a traditional color. The red system is one of self-protection during times of threat or panic. Emotions of fear, anxiety, anger, disgust, and even despair and depression can result from this system. Thus, people are most likely to fight with outbursts or shut down with intent to flee perceived dangers within the red system. Gilbert's blue emotional system is one used for motivation to pursue short-term objectives and long-term goals. The blue system motivates, energizes, and excites. It helps humans solve problems and move forward with positive direction. Finally, the green emotional system is one of care and compassion for others, as well as comfort and security for ourselves. In these moments, humans are grounded in the present moment and fully able to connect with others.

When music educators enter the blue and green emotional stages, they are ready to challenge students and themselves with wholesome learning opportunities. Selecting literature, classroom activities, and performance opportunities that energize and excite is important for successful interactions with students and others. Similarly, the green emotional system allows space for celebration of student and colleague success without jealousy or personal regret. "Capitalizing involves reacting to another person's good news or success stories in a positive, enthusiastic, constructive way. We invite them to talk in detail about their good news and to celebrate their successes in ways that generate positive emotions" (Carr, 2020, p. 220). However, caution should be exercised to avoid overcommitting time and energy to others, where a possibility of compassion fatigue and burnout may result (e.g., Bernhard, 2016; Hedden, 2005).

To negotiate insecure attachment styles (avoidant and anxious), as mentioned in the first half of this chapter, Bowlby (1988) recommended that individuals seek relationships with others who have a more secure background. Working with others who experienced secure childhoods can help provide balance and offset prior trauma. Many school districts have established mentoring programs, in which teachers and leaders with experience and previous success can listen to and encourage those feeling less secure. Personal therapy, both formal and informal, can also be useful in working through insecure attachment challenges. Taking time to slowly and methodically consider past experiences and current dilemmas can help rewrite unhealthy scripts with new alternatives (e.g., Collins & Read, 1990; Wood, 2021).

"Building and maintaining healthy and rewarding relationships with our diverse students and their parents involves clear communication, good listening, cooperation, and skillful conflict resolution skills" (Jennings, 2021, p. 54). Bradford and Robin (2021) supported this notion, outlining their curriculum for developing healthy relationships among Master of Business Administration candidates at Stanford University. They argued that feedback is essential with any couple but clarified that the feedback must remain emotionally connected to the individual who is communicating. Making assumptions about how another person is feeling can lead to inaccuracies and notions of being attacked from the listener. Bradford and Robin used a tennis analogy to suggest that remaining on one's own side of the net is essential to emotional stability and forward progress in any relationship. In a music setting, teachers might assume that administrators or colleagues undervalue their program without sufficient evidence. Similarly, they might assume that students are being rude or lack interest when the root of the problem lies in unspoken frustration and embarrassment over lacking previous knowledge and skill development. Taking a step back to breathe and revisit challenging relationships, often over the course of multiple interactions, can help both sides negotiate for better understanding and can help in the practice of restorative justice.

> Restorative justice empowers students to resolve conflicts on their own and in small groups, and it's a growing practice at schools around the country. Essentially, the idea is to bring students together in peer-mediated small groups to talk, ask questions, and air their grievances.
>
> (Davis, 2015)

While relationships with others are ultimately important, time alone is also essential, particularly for naturally introverted music teachers. Interacting with students and colleagues all day, often six or seven days per week, in a sound-filled environment, can create stress and fatigue. Cain (2013) suggested that introverted individuals must have low-energy quiet spaces for recovery after high-energy interactions with others. Music teachers who are naturally introverted should also be sure to speak up or let their feelings be known in other ways, such as meetings with small groups or responses to email and digital forum conversations. Assuming that your needs are secondary to others, or minimizing the importance of your comments, can lead to frustration and resentment (Bradford & Robin, 2021).

Revisiting the music teacher, Randi, from the beginning of this chapter, let's consider how her life would be improved with better negotiation of human relationships. Randi still teaches a variety of music classes and rehearsals but took the previous summer to focus on general music and choral workshops, both areas that interest her and play to her strengths. The previous year, she presented her building principal with a five-year plan for fiscal budgeting of program growth and asked politely for monthly face-to-face meetings. Randi has enjoyed these meetings and has even learned that the principal enjoys some extracurricular favorites of hers, like bowling. She is learning to objectively present her concerns and the needs of the program, placing student learning at the core of all conversations. The principal has agreed to hire a part-time band instructor, and there are plans for that position to convert to a full-time concert band and modern band teacher the following year, providing further curricular options for all students.

Randi's new level of trust and understanding with the principal, as well as a more reasonable teaching load, help her job enjoyment and self-esteem. She volunteers to lead an after-school bowling league for students and even convinces the principal and some other teachers to participate on occasion. With these new human interactions and developing relationships, Randi finds that she is invited to social gatherings more often, including one that leads to meeting an older colleague's son, who becomes a close personal connection for Randi in the following years. Improved human relationships lead to better choices regarding sleep, physical movement, and nutrition, and while Randi still has moments of stress and challenge, she is enjoying life and developing improved resilience. Instead of avoiding messages from her mother and others, Randi replies with honest feedback about whether she is available to talk or needs quiet time to decompress and rejuvenate. Finally, because Randi is happier with colleagues, family, and close others, she is less jealous of her young students and more available to help them develop appropriately as human beings and musicians.

Summary

- Start with attention to yourself. Embrace sound practices for sleep, physical movement, and nutrition.
- Consider childhood experiences, both positive and challenging, and work with a therapist to address underlying tensions.

- Embrace time with others, particularly face-to-face interactions.
- Practice compassion for others. Consider different perspectives.
- While brief encounters can be beneficial, take time to develop a few deep connections.
- Allow yourself to be vulnerable with a few close relationships. Build deep levels of trust.
- Remain curious, yet emotionally stable, with others. Listen with full intent.
- Seek the best in others, particularly with students. Remember that they might not always be exact replicas of you.
- Let your voice be heard. If uncomfortable in large meetings, share thoughts in smaller groups.
- When possible, keep work and personal relationships separate. Seek community groups and a few close others outside music education.
- If introverted, make space for personal time and hobbies. Create healthy boundaries with any relationship.

References

Bernhard, H. C. (2016). Investigating burnout among elementary and secondary school music educators: A replication. *Contributions to Music Education, 41*, 145–156.

Bernhard, H. C. (2021). *Managing stress in music education: Routes to wellness and vitality.* Routledge.

Bowlby, J. (1988). *A secure base: Clinical implications of attachment theory.* Routledge.

Bradford, D., & Robin, C. (2021). *Connect: Building exceptional relationships with family, friends, and colleagues.* Penguin Books.

Cain, S. (2013). *Quiet: The power of introverts in a world that can't stop talking.* Broadway.

Carr, A. (2020). *Positive psychology and you: A self-development guide.* Routledge.

Collins, N. L., & Read, S. J. (1990). Adult attachment, working models, and relationship quality in dating couples. *Journal of Personality and Social Psychology, 58*(4), 644–663.

Davis, M. (2015). *Restorative justice: Resources for schools.* Retrieved February 21, 2022, from www.edutopia.org/blog/restorative-justice-resources-matt-davis

Gilbert, D. (2021). A comparison of self-reported anxiety and depression among undergraduate music majors and nonmusic majors. *Journal of Music Teacher Education, 30*(3), 69–83.

Gilbert, P. (2010). *Compassion focused therapy: The CBT distinctive features series.* Routledge.

Hedden, D. (2005). A study of stress and its manifestations among music educators. *Bulletin of the Council for Research in Music Education, 166*, 57–67.

Jennings, P. A. (2021). *Teacher burnout turnaround: Strategies for empowered educators.* Norton.

Payne, P. D., Lewis, W., & McCaskill, F. (2020). Looking within: An investigation of music education majors and mental health. *Journal of Music Teacher Education, 29*(3), 50–61.

Rath, T. (2013). *Eat, move, sleep: How small choices lead to big changes.* Missionday.

Roffey, S. (2021). Relationships. In B. Grenville-Cleave, D. Guomundsdottir, F. Huppert, V. King, D. Roffey, S. Roffey, & M. de Vries (Eds.), *Creating the world we want to live in: How positive psychology can build a brighter future* (pp. 91–107). Routledge.

Sindberg, L., & Lipscomb, S. D. (2005). Professional isolation and the public school music teacher. *Bulletin of the Council for Research in Music Education, 166*, 43–56.

Wood, G. W. (2021). *The psychology of wellbeing.* Routledge.

5 Meaning

Patricia is fried. It's the beginning of another fall semester, and she can't quite figure out what became of her summer. She's on an academic hamster wheel, and that wheel is spinning far too fast. Patricia is the head of music education in a small department of music that's housed in a large urban center. While many envy Patricia's city location, she can never find time to take advantage of related cultural offerings because she's always too busy trying to keep up. In addition to her administrative duties within the department, Patricia teaches methods classes for choral and instrumental music education majors, supervises all student teaching placements, and serves as liaison to a large college of education, a position that alone takes more than half of her time and energy. Patricia regularly takes on more than her colleagues, serving as the lone music education representative on most music department committees and publishing an incomprehensible number of journal articles and books each year. She enjoys teaching but feels that college classes might not be her best fit. "If only I could return to the joys of teaching little ones. I so liked my work with elementary school general music, especially the PK–2 students. They were so eager to please, naturally musical, and positive about life!" She anxiously assumes that most college students don't respect her, even though that is not the case, and loses sleep almost every night worrying about upcoming class sessions.

Outside the university, Patricia also keeps a full schedule, caring for her elderly parents from afar and serving on numerous national and international review boards and other professional committees. She assumes that she must call or videoconference with her parents every night and feels tremendous guilt when she considers avoiding such calls. "I better enjoy my parents while they're still here, and I know they don't have anyone else with whom to communicate. Especially since the pandemic started, they don't get out as much as before." Patricia prefers to chat by phone instead of videoconference because it allows her to multitask with article reviews

DOI: 10.4324/9781003331148-5

40 *Meaning*

while she lets her parents talk about their day. This often leads to minor errors in her work, but Patricia figures that as long as she's not the lead editor, the journals will stay afloat and her parents will remain content that their daughter from across the country still loves them.

Psychological meaning is a sense of deep purpose and fulfillment, both professionally and personally. It is what draws human beings to focus on certain career trajectories, styles of interaction with others, and leisure activities (e.g., Bernhard, 2021; Seligman, 2018; Wood, 2021). Psychological meaning tends to be a long-term process and is often reflected upon over the course of a lifetime but can also help create short-term objectives and daily choices (Clear, 2018; Hollis, 2006). Music teachers tend to have strong senses of life meaning, often feeling a certain calling to the profession (e.g., Bernhard, 2020). Miksza et al. (2021) found that even during the COVID-19 pandemic, self-reported psychological meaning was strong for collegiate and K–12 music educators and perhaps was even stronger at the outset of related challenges.

> Educators often commit to teaching as a career because of the intrinsic satisfaction they get from opportunities to work with children and the knowledge they are helping to make a positive difference in the world. . . . As such, it is perhaps not terribly surprising that music educators scored higher than norms for the general population on the meaning scale – even amidst the COVID-19 pandemic.
>
> (pp. 12–13)

Carr (2020) suggested using Seligman and Peterson's (2010) Values in Action Inventory of Strengths (VIA-IS) to determine and reflect upon unique signature strengths that might help clarify psychological meaning on an individual basis. Seligman and Peterson identified 24 values and character strengths from major philosophical traditions around the world and grouped them into six categories – wisdom (creativity, curiosity, judgement, love of learning, and perspective); courage (bravery, perseverance, honesty, and zest); humanity (love, kindness, and social intelligence); justice (teamwork, fairness, and leadership); temperance (forgiveness, humility, prudence, and self-regulation); and transcendence (appreciation of beauty, gratitude, hope, humor, and spirituality). While all 24 values are essential for survival and proper functioning of society, different people thrive in different areas. "A series of randomized controlled trials have shown that identifying your signature strengths with the *VIA-IS*, and then using these strengths regularly, leads to increased well-being and decreased depression" (Carr, 2020, p. 39).

For example, an individual with strong scores in teamwork, fairness, and leadership might be drawn to a successful and rewarding career in administration. Top signature strengths do not necessarily all come from the same categories and, even in a traditional music teaching position, can help provide direction for objectives and goals. A music educator with top signature strengths of gratitude, hope, perspective, and humor might help students and colleagues see (and hear) the big picture. While setbacks in traditional classes and rehearsals can and will occur, maintaining optimism for cumulative growth will remind those in the person's influence to maintain focus on the ultimate purposes of music education. A music educator with top signature strengths of creativity, curiosity, and love of learning might be drawn to more composition and improvisation, even within traditional classes and ensembles. That person might also be a strong team leader, with vision for program growth and curricular innovation.

If the formal process of surveying and analyzing the VIA-IS is initially too much to pursue, Carr (2020) recommended starting with a few more informal activities. Writing or imagining an obituary or memorial service eulogy for yourself can help you clarify life priorities in the present. How do you wish to be remembered? What are your most important values and characteristics in life? Similarly, write a description of your hopes and plans for the next decade, assuming that everything will go as well as possible in the following categories: physical and mental health; relationships with your partner, relationships with your family and friends; achievements in your career at work or in your education; and achievements in leisure activities, sports, and arts (Carr, 2020).

Psychological meaning should be primarily derived from intrinsic motivations, reasons that are important for their own being, as opposed to extrinsic motivations, reasons that are rewarded outside the self (e.g., Seligman, 2018; Wood, 2021). For example, in the preceding exercises, is it important to be remembered as the music teacher who won the most trophies and superior festival ratings in the history of your school, or is it important to be remembered as a teacher who cared deeply about students and promoted lifelong musicianship? Is it most important to be remembered as the teacher who wrote the longest email replies and received the most "likes" on social media or the teacher who connected deeply, in person, with a close network of colleagues? "Pursuing intrinsically rewarding goals fulfills one or more of the most basic human needs.... these include the need for feeling in control, feeling good at what we do, and having good relationships" (Carr, 2020, p. 23).

Intrinsic motivation is not always easy when there is a lack of autonomy. Seligman (2018) wrote about the importance of objectively recognizing what is within our control and what is not. He described a classic study by Langer and Rodin (1976), in which they encouraged autonomy among senior citizens in an assisted living center. The researchers allowed and assisted residents in deciding how furniture would be arranged in their room, choosing their own plants, and determining how they would spend their free time. A control group of participants continued with a traditional practice of externally and pre-planned furniture arrangements, plants, and daily schedules. Not surprisingly, the residents with greater control over their environment were more active physically, had better mental health, and lived longer than their peers. Similarly, Seligman et al. (1995) devised a study in which they taught middle school students to take control of unrealistic pessimistic thoughts and found that treatment group participants were significantly less depressed than those in the control group two years later. "The key to learning optimism is learning how to recognize and then dispute unrealistic catastrophic thoughts" (Seligman, 2018, p. 281).

While music educators will always have some aspects of professional life that are directed by others, particularly as students and early career teachers, there are ways to promote increased autonomy and local decision-making. Good administrators and professors will trust those in their care and encourage independent decision-making. Music educators should advocate for themselves as much as possible, seeking autonomy. This will often require creativity and ingenuity but will be worth the extra effort in terms of psychological engagement and life meaning.

Psychological meaning is also important to consider in leisure activities. For those who feel constricted at work, "leisure activities can be a way of connecting with others, forgetting worries, or doing something meaningful" (Grenville-Cleave & Roffey, 2021, p. 142). While many music educators will choose leisure activities different from the profession, some will benefit from performing groups that allow a higher level of music achievement than is possible in a school setting, perhaps simulating past levels of psychological meaning attained as music majors in university ensembles. Others will enjoy connections with nature, competitive sports, or other social games. Regardless of leisure type, it is important to prioritize such activities, even placing them ahead of work responsibilities at times. "As such, leisure activities can put positive psychology into practice – expressing autonomy, doing something meaningful, improving existing skills, or connecting with others" (Grenville-Cleave & Roffey, 2021, p. 142).

Recommendations for Healthy Psychological Meaning

Using free online generators (e.g., Bouchrika, 2020), analyze word clouds related to text written by yourself and others with whom you work. The resulting visuals can show powerful illustrations of the thought and emotion behind written words. Eichstaedt et al. (2015) employed word clouds to correlate heart health with Twitter posts. With remarkable clarity, they demonstrated that participants from areas of the United States with high rates of cardiovascular death most used terms like "hate, annoying, pissed, and asshole." Word clouds representing Twitter posts of participants from areas with low rates of cardiovascular death tended to use terms like "great, interesting, thanks, and forward." Similarly, Seligman (2018) shared that Twitter posts from neurotic individuals tended to use words like "sick, depressed, nightmare, and angry," while non-neurotic people used words like "workout, beautiful, blessings, and success" (pp. 343–345).

Brainstorm lists of interests and possible career trajectories. My father is fond of saying that if you find a job you enjoy, you'll never have to work a day in your life! Creating a vision board can assist with goal setting and hopeful planning (see Chapter 8). This could be an individual project or a group effort, and there is no one way to go about it. Using a list of goals for the future, draw, photograph, or source images from places like newspapers and magazines (Regan, 2021). Carr (2020) suggested that related goals be

> Collaborative – involve working cooperatively with others; Limited – in both scope and duration; Emotional – in that they are valued and involve a high level of commitment; Appreciable – insofar as they can be subdivided into smaller goals if necessary; Refinable – in that they may be modified in light of changing circumstances.
>
> (p. 32)

Seek autonomy and recognize that students and colleagues may have different goals for life meaning. While it is obviously necessary to work with others in most music-making or education environments, planning for scenarios where a sense of control can be attained is important for both teachers and learners. Schedule brief and meaningful meetings with administrators to demonstrate why some autonomy in curricular direction is needed. As one of my favorite collegiate administrators once said, "Hire good people and let them do their jobs." In the same vein, students should be allowed and encouraged to have some degree of choice in the learning process. Presenting a few carefully culled literature selections and allowing student vote (or individual choice for solo study) can help provide autonomy. It can also be a powerful learning opportunity when students are encouraged to discuss why they have made certain decisions.

Recognize that some aspects of the music education profession, and life, will be out of one's control. Mundane administrative tasks such as general email replies, faculty meetings, and bus/lunch duties will likely be a required component of any music teaching position. But if these can be limited and completed mindfully, they can maintain an appropriate balance of attention without overwhelming or taking away from more meaningful parts of the job. Choose one or two times per day to answer email, perhaps limited by a timer, and select only the most pressing meetings to attend, without leading unnecessary gatherings, yourself. Qualman (2020) described the career successes of Warren Buffet, pointing out that Buffet focused on projects that were within his realm of expertise while leaving other opportunities to peers. "To stack the odds in his favor, he kept his center of competence and, in baseball terms, swung for the fences on a few investment decisions that he was most certain about, then held them for the long term" (p. 65).

Strive for meaning in both your professional and leisure time. While it's important to find work that will both make a positive difference and play to your strengths, it is equally essential to participate in leisure activities that are rewarding and psychologically meaningful. While some music teachers may find meaning in further music-making or teaching activities beyond the traditional school day, it is more likely that they might find deep fulfilment in service to a community organization, participation in physical activity, or creation of art outside the realm of music. A friend of mine finds great relaxation, yet still with focus and meaning, in the art of pottery. He relishes the opportunity to interact with people who are not professional music educators, play with clay and fire, and share finished products with family and friends.

Ikigai is a Japanese tradition of finding meaning in life. It is often translated in Western realms to finding meaning in careers or other professional venues (e.g., Eatough, 2021). But Wood (2021) suggested that it is even more important to find a work-life balance in which ikigai and other concepts of psychological meaning are honed in personal settings. When searching for related activities, he recommended "starting small (goals); releasing (accepting) yourself; finding harmony and sustainability (socially and environmentally); appreciating the joy of little things; and being in the here and now (mindfulness)" (p. 87). As with work settings, making a list of what not to do could be useful in leisure activities. What habits and thoughts drain time and energy, and how might they be released or mitigated to create space for a more meaningful use of personal time?

Revisiting the college professor, Patricia, from the beginning of this chapter, let's consider how her life would be improved with healthy adjustments to psychological meaning. Patricia composes a list and vision board of life priorities and decides to start with personal issues, realizing that those might ultimately be more important than work challenges. While Patricia does love her parents very much, she reaches out to her two siblings to determine whether they might be able to help. "We didn't realize Mom and Dad needed so much attention," one of her sisters responded. "Yeah, Mother and Father have actually asked me to cut back on communications so that they can visit their neighbors more often," added her brother. This was news to Patricia, but when she gently asked her parents for more information, they shyly confirmed the story. "We didn't want to offend you, Patty, but it would honestly work better for us if we just check in once per week." Patricia had automatically assumed that everyone needed her attention all the time but now realized that she was the one who had initiated daily contact. What a relief it was to suddenly gain ten hours per week instead of multitasking while listening to her parents try to appease her with daily stories!

Patricia similarly cuts back on professional service to just one journal review board. Because she can now better focus, she even agrees to serve as associate to the editor. While this involves a bit more work, Patricia finds that she now enjoys the entire process more fully, understanding the comprehensive package of journal content, instead of just randomly and halfheartedly participating in numerous reviews of unrelated manuscripts. This increase in psychological meaning also helps Patricia realize that her own list of publications would have a more positive impact with a shift from quantity to quality. Patricia aims for and easily accomplishes one meaningful peer-reviewed publication per academic year, providing space for her to read more (even for pleasure!), take advantage of local cultural offerings like art museums and film festivals, and more deeply enjoy the company of a few close friends.

The shift also allows Patricia to slow her pace of teaching and service on her own campus, again dialing back on quantity while improving quality. After a series of meetings with school administrators, Patricia develops a plan in which a second tenure-track music education colleague can join her in two years. That colleague will teach all instrumental music methods courses and take half of Patricia's student teaching supervisions and committee assignments. Patricia chooses to focus on elementary general music methods and now has time to start a meaningful partnership with the local community children's center. She is so excited about working with the little ones again, and that positive energy transfers easily to undergraduate music education majors, who had always respected Patricia but now adore her and often cite her as their most meaningful influence when reflecting as alumni of the music education program.

Summary

- Create a list of interests, signature strengths, and important values in life.
- Consider whether these interests, strengths, and values are being highlighted at work.
- Remind yourself why you love teaching and making music.
- Focus on changes that are within your control, recognizing that a small portion of your day may be scheduled by others. Value and consider their perspectives and values.
- Create a vision board. Choose pictures and other items that represent a meaningful future.
- Strive for healthy work-life balance by focusing on meaningful leisure activities and leaving work at school.

Meaning 47

- Make a not-to-do list, for both work and home.
- Meet with friends and colleagues to exchange ideas about concerns and hopes.
- Allow yourself to be vulnerable with a few close relationships. Build deep levels of trust.
- Remain calm when setbacks occur. Practice gratitude and remember all that is well.

References

Bernhard, H. C. (2020). An investigation of happiness and gratitude among music educators. *Visions of Research in Music Education, 36*, 1–15.

Bernhard, H. C. (2021). *Managing stress in music education: Routes to wellness and vitality*. Routledge.

Bouchrika, I. (2020). *7 best word cloud generator tools for school and work*. Retrieved January 30, 2022, from https://research.com/software/best-word-cloud-generators

Carr, A. (2020). *Positive psychology and you: A self-development guide*. Routledge.

Clear, J. (2018). *Atomic habits: An easy and proven way to build good habits and break bad ones*. Avery.

Eatough, S. (2021). *What is ikigai and how can it change my life?* Retrieved January 31, 2022, from www.betterup.com/blog/what-is-ikigai

Eichstaedt, J. C., Schwartz, H. A., Kern, M. L., Park, G., Labarthe, D. R., Merchant, R. M., & Seligman, M. E. (2015). Psychological language on Twitter predicts county-level heart disease mortality. *Psychological Science, 26*(2), 159–169.

Grenville-Cleave, B., & Roffey, S. (2021). Leisure. In B. Grenville-Cleave, D. Guomundsdottir, F. Huppert, V. King, D. Roffey, S. Roffey, & M. de Vries (Eds.), *Creating the world we want to live in: How positive psychology can build a brighter future* (pp. 141–153). Routledge.

Hollis, J. (2006). *Finding meaning in the second half of life: How to finally, really grow up*. Avery.

Langer, E. J., & Rodin, J. (1976). The effects of choice and enhanced personal responsibility for the aged: A field experiment in an institutional setting. *Journal of Personality and Social Psychology, 34*(2), 191–198.

Miksza, P., Parkes, K., Russell, J. A., & Bauer, W. (2021). The well-being of music educators during the pandemic: Spring of 2020. *Psychology of Music*, 1–17.

Qualman, E. (2020). *The focus project: How to focus in an unfocused world*. Equalman Studios.

Regan, S. (2021). *How vision boards work and how to make a powerful one for yourself*. Retrieved January 7, 2022, from www.mindbodygreen.com/articles/how-to-make-a-vision-board

Seligman, M. E. P. (2018). *The hope circuit: A psychologist's journey from helplessness to optimism*. Public Affairs.

Seligman, M. E. P., Gillham, J., Jaycox, L., & Reivich, K. (1995). *The optimistic child: A proven program to safeguard children against depression and build lifelong resistance.* Harper Perennial.
Seligman, M. E. P., & Peterson, C. (2010). *The VIA character strengths survey.* Retrieved January 28, 2022, from www.viacharacter.org/survey/account/register
Wood, G. W. (2021). *The psychology of wellbeing.* Routledge.

6 Accomplishment

Harry can't stand how bad his band sounds. After placing second in numerous national and international orchestral auditions, he reluctantly accepted the job of band director at a local high school. Instead of offering any sound advice for improvement, he simply whips out his trumpet and plays along with the group, as loud and as high as possible. When a tuba player who has been diagnosed with attention deficit hyperactivity disorder disrupts class by chatting with a nearby peer, Harry screams at him and stops rehearsal to give everyone another lecture about proper rehearsal etiquette. "If any of you truly understood real musicianship, you would focus and play better. This is just a lost cause!" He glares at the tuba player and tells him to get out of the room immediately. When the student asks where he should go, Harry sarcastically replies, "Like I care. Go play in traffic!" The remaining students are scared and untrusting of their teacher and are increasingly visiting the high school counselor in an effort to change course schedules.

Harry was a trumpet major in college, earning bachelor's and master's performance degrees from distinguished music conservatories. His two older brothers also graduated from these institutions, and both now hold prestigious positions in internationally renowned professional orchestras. Harry feels jilted, and ultimately embarrassed, that he has not successfully followed in their footsteps. Instead of being happy and proud of his siblings, Harry stops communicating with them and instead rants on social media about how unfair the world is. "Here's another video of my 'amazing' brother performing with his 'amazing' orchestra. Everyone knows that I should be the one on that stage. I'll have to take my talents some place where they're actually appreciated!"

Still, Harry is recognized as a highly skilled trumpet performer and is hired regularly by community churches and civic groups, and he serves as guest clinician for many local institutions. At a recent engagement with a nearby community college, Harry performs an impressive recital, followed

DOI: 10.4324/9781003331148-6

50 *Accomplishment*

by a master class with three trumpet majors. But instead of actually helping the students, Harry takes the opportunity to denigrate their performances and promote himself. "It's Mickey Mouse people like you who give solo brass performance a bad name," he quips to one student. "Turn your stand around and play this movement from memory." When the student turns red from embarrassment and fails to play even the opening measures, Harry simply chuckles, turns to the audience, and says, "They don't make trumpet players like me anymore!"

Harry has many impressive accomplishments in his life but fails to recognize many of them, instead comparing himself to others and assuming that he should have more. While the formal field of positive psychology is only a couple of decades old, scholars have long posited that healthy appreciation for personal accomplishment is important. Christina Maslach and colleagues began studying the construct of burnout in the 1970s and found that people who struggled in the helping professions tended to display high levels of emotional exhaustion and depersonalization while also displaying low recognition of personal accomplishment (Maslach et al., 1983). In the Educators Survey of the Maslach Burnout Inventory, statements such as "I have accomplished many worthwhile things in my teaching career; I feel I'm positively influencing other people's lives through my work; I feel exhilarated after working closely with my students and colleagues" represent personal accomplishment (Maslach et al., 1983, p. 1). Participants who feel these statements to be true on a frequent basis are considered to be psychologically healthy, while those who do not feel them on a regular basis are considered to be either headed toward or already suffering from psychological burnout.

More recently, Martin Seligman and colleagues included accomplishment as a primary component of their PERMA model of human flourishing, positing that psychologically healthy individuals display strong practices related to positive emotion, engagement, relationships, meaning, and accomplishment. "These accomplishments may include completing daily tasks and responsibilities, reaching goals, achieving success, and winning. They may be in the domains of work or leisure activities" (Carr, 2020, p. 7). Butler and Kern (2015) created a PERMA profiler, in which the following three questions measure psychological accomplishment: "How much of the time do you feel you are making progress towards accomplishing your goals? How often do you achieve the important goals you have set for yourself? How often are you able to handle your responsibilities?" (p. 1).

Miksza et al. (2021) used the PERMA profiler with 2,023 music teachers during the first part of the COVID-19 pandemic, in the spring of 2020. Regarding accomplishment, they found that collective participant responses were significantly lower than published norms and that perceptions of accomplishment lessened in relation to collegiate degree earned (i.e., participants with only a bachelor's degree reported significantly lower levels of accomplishment than those with master's, and those with a master's reported significantly lower levels of accomplishment than those with doctoral degrees). The same researchers later investigated the impacts of the COVID-19 pandemic on K–12 music teachers at the beginning of the next school year, fall 2020. Again using the PERMA profiler as one measure, they collected data from 1,325 educators and found that "overall, the participants reported poorer well-being than published norms and the sample of participants in our previous study" (Parkes et al., 2021, p. 2837).

Carr (2020) suggested that genetic and environmental challenges may influence feelings of accomplishment, such that some individuals are more naturally predisposed for success. Citing earlier research of Lyubomirsky (2007), he cautioned that genetic factors can differentiate perceptions of accomplishment among differing personality traits. "A large body of research shows that extraversion, emotional stability, conscientiousness, and agreeableness are associated with more satisfying relationships, better work performance and job satisfaction, healthier lifestyles, and more adaptive coping with stress and adversity" (Carr, 2020, p. 13).

Similarly, Argyle (2001) and Clark et al. (2018) found that environmental circumstances can influence one's ability to healthily perceive accomplishments. They suggested that supportive relationships, sufficient finances, and personal autonomy were all important to healthy perceptions of accomplishment. Regarding financial means, they cautioned that once basic needs are met, too much wealth can have an inverse effect on well-being and success. These researchers also found that physical health and sufficient living quarters were important environmental factors and that females younger than 30 or older than 50 tended to have healthier perceptions of accomplishment than other genders or ages. Carr (2020), however, reminded readers that "the personal and circumstantial factors listed above only account for about 10% of the long-lasting happiness people experience" (p. 15).

Imposter syndrome is a psychological condition in which individuals might be performing at an acceptable or even very strong level but perceive that they are not worthy of success or that they are frauds who will soon be exposed for their perceived weaknesses. Sims and Cassidy (2020) reported high levels of impostor syndrome among music education graduate students, as measured by the Clance Impostor Phenomenon Scale, and that associated feelings were stronger in females and those who were the first in their family to attend graduate school. Imposter syndrome is often related to perfectionism, in which individuals perceive the need to avoid mistakes at all costs. Younger students can also feel imposter syndrome, and music teachers should help ameliorate this possibility by creating a warm and welcoming environment in which risk-taking is encouraged and regular support is provided.

From an opposite perspective, it is also unhealthy to feel too confident about accomplishments, resulting in narcissistic behavior. While narcissists tend to focus on themselves and have a strong sense of confidence, such behavior is often rooted in insecurity and concern about the perception of others. Social media and other digital forms of sharing make it very easy for narcissistic behavior to readily be displayed. Goncalo et al. (2010) examined connections between narcissism and creativity and found that "narcissists are not necessarily more creative than others, but they think they are, and they are adept at persuading others to agree with them" (p. 1484). Music educators can help overly confident students by offering greater challenges, sharing examples of or perhaps working with stronger performers, and helping students develop a sense of humility and empathy for others.

Despite these potential challenges, recognition of personal accomplishment is an important component of cumulative psychological well-being. Once a healthy balance of self-recognition has been achieved, it is also important to help students enjoy appreciation of accomplishments, both from a personal and a communal perspective. Students often have different ideas about accomplishment than do their teachers, both overestimating and underestimating their performances. During my years as a middle school teacher, I often had to help students recognize that, despite their collective bravado, there was still much work to be done before concert performance. On the contrary, I now work with many collegiate music education majors who give up on themselves too easily and can only talk or write about weaknesses in their musicianship and teaching ability. Helping students celebrate strengths on a regular basis, while also keeping areas for growth in mind, can help provide a healthy balance for lifelong learning and growth (e.g., Bernhard, 2021; Bono, 2020; Seligman, 2018; Wood, 2021).

Recommendations for Healthy Recognition of Accomplishment

Start by recognizing past accomplishments and efforts. Particularly during times of stress and uncertainty, it's easy to forget or undervalue past achievements (e.g., Carr, 2020; Wood, 2021). Humans instead tend to catastrophize with anxiety and doubt about perceived future troubles. By recognizing past instances of grit and resilience, whether personal or communal, and whether within music education or outside, it's possible to garner hope for the future (e.g., Goodall et al., 2021; Gwinn & Hellman, 2019; Lopez, 2014; Seligman, 2018). While trophies, plaques, and other external signs of recognition should be displayed with caution, pride and remembrance of past achievements can often provide motivation for the future. Even if the same students are not still present, school and music program esprit de corps can be manifested when facilitated with care.

Similarly, stack habits for success and accomplishment. If one task or event is already occurring well, use it as a cue for something else. This could be as simple as a welcome song leading to appropriate seating in an elementary general music class or the sound of a tuning note leading to focus at the beginning of an ensemble rehearsal. In personal settings, this could be something like feeding a pet each morning followed by five minutes of mindful meditation or brushing teeth followed by listing three items of gratitude.

> The key is to tie your desired behavior into something you already do each day. Once you have mastered this basic structure, you can begin to create larger stacks by chaining small habits together. This allows you to take advantage of the natural momentum that comes from one behavior leading into the next.
>
> (Clear, 2018, pp. 74–75)

Work in small chunks. When starting the process of writing this book, it was a bit daunting to look at blinking cursors and blank pages, fretting over eight chapters yet to be written. But by making a daily habit of writing first thing each morning, and giving myself permission to write anything and edit later, sentences were constructed, paragraphs took form, and a full book is now close to completion (this is the final chapter being composed). With other tasks, I also make a habit of working early, focusing on high-concentration goals early in the day and leaving more easy and pleasurable activities for later. Remembering that physical movement will usually improve my mood and productivity, I also make a point of running or biking a short amount before teaching classes or interacting with others. "It is so easy to overestimate the importance of one defining moment and underestimate the value of making small improvements on a daily basis" (Clear, 2018, p. 15).

Use caution when making comparisons with others. In addition to academic content and learning, school cultures play an important role in developing social skills. Children, and even teachers, are adept at worrying whether they measure acceptably compared to others. This pressure is compounded by social media and other Internet resources. Descriptors and visual images of seemingly perfect lives can make it difficult to focus on healthy levels of accomplishment and thus can lead to feelings of depression or anxiety (e.g., Diener & Biswas-Diener, 2008; Lyubomirsky, 2007; Seligman, 2011). While sharing accomplishments on social media and other venues can be a positive source of pride and program advocacy, care must be practiced to maintain kindness and healthy awareness of others.

> Rather than children worrying about being richer, cleverer, or better looking than other people, perhaps families could stress what we have in common, and show compassion for those who fall on hard times.

Kindness boosts a positive self-concept and having a sense of meaning beyond the self can lead to a life well lived.

(Roffey, 2021, p. 28)

Celebrate accomplishments in both school and personal contexts. While success is often measured and compared in professional settings, accomplishments in leisure settings and fields outside of music are also important to recognize (e.g., Grenville-Cleave & Roffey, 2021; King & Huppert, 2021). For example, completing a couch-to-5K running event or month-long streak of clean eating can provide motivation for professional success. Similarly, students who are challenged by music might excel at classes and events in other school areas and vice versa. I once worked with a high school cellist who struggled to maintain focus and make progress in our traditional orchestra ensemble. But he was a state finalist in the shot put event of track and field. When I happened to see his name in the local newspaper sports page, right next to a picture of Michael Jordan, I saved the article and shared it with him during our next rehearsal. While his cello performance didn't immediately improve, the student did appreciate being positively recognized in front of his peers and gave much greater effort during rehearsals for the next several weeks.

Create an environment conducive to accomplishment. Clear (2018) suggested that habits and organized surroundings are important prerequisites to success. "Habits are like the entrance ramp to a highway. They lead you down a path and, before you know it, you're speeding toward the next behavior" (p. 160). At home, positive habits and environments might include setting workout or school clothes in ready position for the next morning before going to bed. If cold weather is a deterrent to heading out the door, leave clothes near the dryer so they can be briefly warmed before going outside. Similarly, making your bed each morning, at least pulling sheets and blankets to an organized position, can help with quality of sleep the following night. At school, positive environments conducive to accomplishment might include simple and decluttered pathways to chairs, folders, instruments, and other equipment such that students can easily prepare for class or rehearsal. While posters, smartboards, and other visuals can be useful for motivation, cull the content and appearance for efficiency and productivity.

Revisiting the music teacher, Harry, from the beginning of this chapter, let's consider how his life would be improved with healthy adjustments to psychological accomplishment. Harry smiles warmly as students enter the high school rehearsal space. He chats with individual students as they take their places and welcomes the group with a brief mindfulness breathing activity. The band slowly warms up, and Harry praises their tone quality and progress over the past few weeks. When a tuba player seems distracted and seeks attention from his peers, Harry invites the student to the podium to serve as guest adjudicator for the next piece. "Jason, you have such a good ear for bass lines in this ensemble. Let's have you provide feedback to the other low brass, timpani, bassoons, bass clarinet, and bari sax, but I also want you to listen for melodic lines. Tell us which groups you hear playing the melody as we rehearse this next section." Jason loves the attention and makes astute observations, which his peers also appreciate and use to broaden their understandings of ensemble balance and blend.

After a successful and enjoyable school day, Harry takes a moment to pop onto social media, seeing a new post from one of his brothers. Instead of feeling resentful or angry, Harry reshares the post with a new message, "This is one of my awesome brothers with his outstanding orchestra. I am humbled every time I hear him. All the love, bro!" Harry later heads over to the local community college for a master class with a few trumpet majors. When the first student appears nervous and flustered by the opportunity, Harry gently stops him and starts with praise. "Wow, such courage to perform in front of this full house in your beautiful recital hall. I love the way you played that opening and am kind of jealous of your nice embouchure. Now, take a deep breath, relax, and let's work on this middle section." The student laughs, exhales a sigh of relief, and enjoys the rest of his session with Harry. Afterward, the entire trumpet studio gathers around, chatting informally with Harry and requesting a group selfie to post on their studio social media site. They tag Harry's account on the post, with the description, "Best trumpet teacher ever!" Harry finishes the day by attending an orchestra concert featuring one of his brothers. He sits in the middle of the auditorium, not seeking attention but enjoying his role as an audience member, soaking in the sounds and appreciating the goodness of the moment.

Summary

- Write a list of accomplishments. Recognize how far you've already come.
- Stack successes, building on previous achievements.
- Create an environment conducive to accomplishment.
- Share achievements with others, but avoid narcissistic overload.
- Recognize accomplishment in both professional and personal settings.
- Meet with a trusted friend to compare your perceptions with theirs.
- Monitor potential imposter syndrome.
- Be careful when making comparisons with others.
- Focus on meaningful, intrinsic accomplishment instead of meaningless, extrinsic trophies and plaques.

- Recognize that accomplishment can be a communal effort. You don't have to do it all.
- Write short-term and long-term goals. Use a planner to organize ideas.
- Work in small chunks. Baby steps lead to giant leaps.
- Remain curious and practice lifelong learning.

References

Argyle, M. (2001). *The psychology of happiness*. Routledge.
Bernhard, H. C. (2021). *Managing stress in music education: Routes to wellness and vitality*. Routledge.
Bono, T. (2020). *Happiness 101: Simple secrets to smart living and well-being*. Grand Central.
Butler, J., & Kern, M. L. (2015). *The PERMA profiler: A brief multidimensional measure of flourishing*. Kern Publications.
Carr, A. (2020). *Positive psychology and you: A self-development guide*. Routledge.
Clark, A., Fleche, S., Layard, R., Powdthavee, N., & Ward, G. (2018). *The origins of happiness: The science of well-being over the life course*. Princeton University Press.
Clear, J. (2018). *Atomic habits: An easy and proven way to build good habits and break bad ones*. Avery.
Diener, E., & Biswas-Diener, R. (2008). *Happiness: Unlocking the mysteries of psychological wealth*. Blackwell.
Goncalo, J. A., Flynn, F. J., & Kim, S. H. (2010). Are two narcissists better than one? The link between narcissism, perceived creativity, and creative performance. *Personality and Social Psychology Bulletin, 36*(11), 1484–1495.
Goodall, J., Abrams, D., & Hudson, G. (2021). *The book of hope: A survival guide for trying times*. Celadon Books.
Grenville-Cleave, B., & Roffey, S. (2021). Leisure. In B. Grenville-Cleave, D. Guomundsdottir, F. Huppert, V. King, D. Roffey, S. Roffey, & M. de Vries (Eds.), *Creating the world we want to live in: How positive psychology can build a brighter future* (pp. 141–153). Routledge.
Gwinn, C., & Hellman, C. (2019). *Hope rising: How the science of HOPE can change your life*. Morgan James.
King, V., & Huppert, F. (2021). Foundations for a brighter future. In B. Grenville-Cleave, D. Guomundsdottir, F. Huppert, V. King, D. Roffey, S. Roffey, & M. de Vries (Eds.), *Creating the world we want to live in: How positive psychology can build a brighter future* (pp. 3–19). Routledge.
Lopez, S. (2014). *Making hope happen: Creating the future you want for yourself and others*. Atria.
Lyubomirsky, S. (2007). *The how of happiness*. Penguin.
Maslach, C., Jackson, S. E., & Leiter, M. P. (1983). *Maslach burnout inventory – manual*. College of California Consulting Psychologists Press.
Miksza, P., Parkes, K., Russell, J. A., & Bauer, W. (2021). The well-being of music educators during the pandemic: Spring of 2020. *Psychology of Music*, 1–17.

Parkes, K. A., Russell, J. A., Bauer, W. I., & Miksza, P. (2021). The well-being and instructional experiences of K-12 music educators: Starting a new school year during a pandemic. *Frontiers in Psychology*, 2837.
Roffey, S. (2021). Childhood. In B. Grenville-Cleave, D. Guomundsdottir, F. Huppert, V. King, D. Roffey, S. Roffey, & M. de Vries (Eds.), *Creating the world we want to live in: How positive psychology can build a brighter future* (pp. 23–37). Routledge.
Seligman, M. E. P. (2011). *Flourish: A visionary new understanding of happiness and well-being.* Simon and Schuster.
Seligman, M. E. P. (2018). *The hope circuit: A psychologist's journey from helplessness to optimism.* Public Affairs.
Sims, W. L., & Cassidy, J. W. (2020). Impostor feelings of music education graduate students. *Journal of Research in Music Education, 68*(3), 249–263.
Wood, G. W. (2021). *The psychology of wellbeing.* Routledge.

7 Resilience

Born female but questioning gender feelings, Ari is a sophomore sound recording technology major in a large school of music. They feel generally supported by peers at the university but must go by "Arianna" whenever communicating with their mother, which has become a three-times-daily event. In addition to this frustration and sadness, Ari longs to be a music education major. They had started with this plan as a freshman but experienced

DOI: 10.4324/9781003331148-7

a challenging early field experience at a local middle school and were thus advised by an impatient field supervisor to immediately switch majors. Ari had initially felt that their band rehearsal was going well but noticed that a percussionist in the back of the room was smirking and failing to play along as assigned. Instead of calmly asking the student whether everything was okay (the student was confused about which mallets to use), Ari assumed that he was laughing at their new pantsuit. Ari wanted to explore a more masculine teacher presentation and asked the field supervisor whether they could use the salutation "Mx." instead of "Ms." Struggling with the denial of that request, and insecure about the new pantsuit and lack of teaching experience, Ari lashed out at the percussion student, causing all the middle schoolers to feel alarmed and uncomfortable. After class, instead of calmly engaging in conversation, the field supervisor, who did not know Ari well, demanded that they switch majors because "she" was obviously not a good fit for music education.

The final straw for Ari was a struggle with music theory classes. Like their sound recording technology major, Ari feels uncomfortable with mathematical explanations of music in theory. They thrive at horn performance and aural skills but never did well with high school science and math and assume that they are destined to fail at anything related. Ari feels helpless and doesn't know where to start. They lose sleep every night and lack interest in eating. Their friends invite Ari to take walks and play pick-up games of basketball, but Ari instead chooses to sullenly stare out their dorm room window. Ari lacks resilience, unsure about how challenges should be addressed or how any sort of forward progress might be made. Instead of mindfully calming thoughts, anxiety builds, and Ari spins with negativity and sadness.

When asked whether she had any hope for the future amidst the COVID-19 pandemic, climate change, and social ills, Jane Goodall calmly responded that she felt action was needed but she did indeed believe in good (Goodall et al., 2021). Among her reasons for optimism, Goodall cited the resilience of nature and the indomitable human spirit. Regarding nature, she discussed cycles of seasons and rebirth of trees, plants, and other flora. She described impressive underground networks of tree roots designed to protect and communicate with one another. Two particular cases of tree resilience deserve further attention. After the tragic events of September 11, 2001, in New York City, a withered tree root and sad set of attached branches were found at the site of Ground Zero. Instead of disposing of them along with other ruins, a worker thought that the remains might still be alive and started a process of rehabilitating the tree. Miraculously, the tree responded positively, flourishing and now standing as a somber but resilient "Survivor Tree" at Ground Zero. Similarly, a tree root that survived the horrific atomic bombing of Nagasaki, Japan, during World War II has regenerated and now stands as a healthy, yet scarred, reminder of natural resilience.

Humans, too, have demonstrated incredible resilience over the course of time, something Goodall described as the indomitable human spirit. One of her examples is Chris Koch, a Canadian man who was born with no arms or legs. Despite these obvious challenges, he is happy, positive, and resilient. "He travels around on a long board – and there is virtually nothing he can't do. He travels the world, goes in for marathons, drives tractors – and is an excellent inspirational speaker" (Goodall et al., 2021, pp. 151–152). In the example from the beginning of this chapter, Ari is experiencing definite challenges, but none so extreme that resilience cannot be found. With calm awareness and planning, Ari can find ways to flourish.

Goodall also suggested that adaptation is an essential part of resilience. During the pandemic, successful music educators have adapted and adjusted to overcome challenges, and many have even found benefits and new opportunities. Technology has been embraced by many, providing access for individual recordings to be combined for final performance. While some lamented the loss of live performance, local teachers used the opportunity to invite program alumni, parents, and community members to join in music making, even if participating from far away. Those who successfully adapted to the pandemic also demonstrated great empathy and kindness, sharing materials and ideas, collaborating openly, and otherwise assisting as needed. For example, one university alumnus recognized the need for field experience at his alma mater and thus created a Google Meet platform for his high school students to interact with music education majors. He described the resulting communications as being even better than traditional field experiences, allowing all his high school students to partner with a variety of undergraduate personalities and instrument specialties.

Mindfulness can also help develop resilience (e.g., Davidson, 2012; Hawkins, 2017; Seligman, 2018; Srinivasan, 2014). Observing thoughts from an outsider's perspective, objectively and calmly noticing rather than being yanked impulsively from one reaction to the next, can aid in protecting biological and psychological functioning in the face of threats, whether perceived or real. Mindfulness also helps with confidence and equanimity. During stressful moments, the ability to breathe calmly and remain centered can help with assurance that past planning has been sound. "These values and inner awareness prevent us from being puppets. Sure, paying attention requires work and awareness, but isn't that better than being jerked about on a string?" (Holiday & Hanselman, 2016, p. 22).

From this place of mindful awareness, psychological grit and a growth mindset can occur. A growth mindset is a state of trusting that learning is a lifelong process and that room always exists for improvement and progress, both personal and communal (Carr, 2020; Dweck, 2007; King & Huppert, 2021; Wood, 2021). As opposed to a fixed mindset, in which students or teachers might believe that they are destined to unwanted places or outcomes, a growth mindset encourages resilience to power through with a belief that certain desired outcomes have simply not yet happened.

> If we see difficulties and failures as part of the learning process, we are more likely to grow in our capabilities, whereas if we see them as a sign of incompetence or lack of ability, we avoid seeking challenges and our learning is limited.
>
> (King & Huppert, 2021, p. 9)

From this perspective, rehearsals or practice sessions that don't go as planned are not the end of the world. Students or teachers who have a bad day or don't demonstrate skills and knowledge as initially planned are not deemed disasters or lost causes. Growth mindset and resilience go hand in hand to motivate for positive transformation, even if that state may be in the future (e.g., Clear, 2018; Duhigg, 2014; Dweck, 2007).

Grit is a psychological trait toward hard work and determination. Duckworth (2016) argued that aptitude alone is not enough for success and that labels of "talent" might actually be detrimental to learning and school success. Instead, she coined the term "grit," suggesting that teachers help students hone capacities for deep focus and resilience. "The 'naturalness bias' is a hidden prejudice against those who've achieved what they have because they worked for it, and a hidden preference for those whom we think arrived at their place in life because they're naturally talented" (Duckworth, 2016, p. 25). Traditional music choirs, orchestras, and concert bands unfortunately follow this model too often. Entry points occur only in early grades, and students who are not able to participate or do not follow traditional expectations of musical "talent" are left behind, leaving only 10%–15% of traditional high school students remaining. In contrast, some newer models of music education, such as modern band and song writing, allow space for Duckworth's notion of grit and result in more sustainable student participation, both in terms of quantity and quality (e.g., Powell & Burstein, 2017).

Recommendations for Building Resilience

Professional basketball players are well known for their ability, or lack thereof, to rebound. The best rebounders are sometimes those who find their own missed shots, realizing early where a stray attempt might land. Similarly, in the game of baseball, a successful hitter records an out during 70% of at bats. While it is not necessary to fully embrace failure, we must make contingency plans for times when things do not go as expected. Teaching music is a messy and complex process, involving human interactions, unplanned challenges, and non-linear progress. Leaving extra time for concert preparation or goal attainment can allow space for unexpected setbacks and can provide opportunity for welcome deviations. For example, extra time in a traditional concert preparation cycle can provide space for creative exploration of improvisation or composition, interpersonal exchanges with students, and resilient repair of plans that go awry (e.g., Aguilar, 2018; Harris, 2020).

To further aid in resilience, Jennings (2021) described five competencies teachers need to develop and maintain for effective social and emotional negotiations in a school climate: self-awareness, self-management, social awareness, relationship skills, and effective decision-making. "Supporting teachers' social and emotional development results in improvements not only in teachers' own well-being and functioning but also in the quality of their classroom interactions and student engagement" (Jennings, 2021, pp. 43–44).

Self-awareness helps educators objectively study their own learning styles, personality types, and inherent biases. Recognizing these scripts or default parameters creates protection against automatic "fight or flight" reactions during moments of pressure. For music teachers, this reflection might include considering why certain literature is programmed, how they respond to student behavior issues, and whether hidden curriculum policies are unknowingly in place. Similarly, self-management includes ways in which teachers respond. In stressful situations, healthy self-management provides space for honest response instead of stifling frustrations or reacting uncontrollably.

> Self-management also involves the way we organize our time, our activities, and our surroundings. Do I put things off to finish them at the last minute? . . . Do I have a self-care routine? . . . Do I take on more than I have the capacity to accomplish?
> (Jennings, 2021, p. 52)

Social awareness involves how our students, colleagues, and others may differ from our own background, considering cultural differences regarding race, ethnicity, gender, religion, music preference, etc. This awareness requires open-mindedness and intentional study about the inequities and social hierarchies inherent in a typical school environment. For example, a music teacher might invite students to help with repertoire selection and provide space for them to teach and lead by mixing seating arrangements, presenting a special topic, or serving as a section leader for the day. This awareness can lead to improved relationship skills (see Chapter 4) and responsible decision-making. "While we may have the expertise and training to be a 'warm demander' – the mode science has shown works best when it comes to managing behavior – our stress can get in the way" (Jennings, 2021, p. 57).

Jennings (2015) suggested that mindfulness can help develop and hone these five social and emotional teacher competencies, as well as overall life resilience. Practice informal mindfulness during daily interactions and formal mindfulness during moments of calm and rest. While time and space for formal meditation may be limited, it is important to occasionally, yet regularly, practice this skill to aid in daily moments of mindfulness. Even five to ten minutes of focus on the breath before sleeping or after waking can help you reflect and set intentions for the day. When longer stretches of time are available, a formal meditation like the body scan that follows can be practiced.

> Begin by bringing awareness to the bottoms of your feet as you notice the feeling of your feet resting against the floor. Perhaps you notice pressure where your feet make contact with the floor, or the touch of your socks on your skin. Maybe you notice tingling or other sensations, or maybe you don't notice much sensation at all. It makes no difference; you are not trying to change anything, just to see what is actually happening in this moment. As you continue to watch the sensations in your feet, allow yourself to become aware of your breath moving in and out of your body. If it seems helpful, try to imagine your breath moving in and out through the bottoms of your feet. With each in-breath, allow your awareness to sharpen; with each out-breath, allow tension and tightness to be released from your feet. Breathing in, focus your attention; breathing out, release tension. After a minute or so, move your awareness up to your lower legs. With an attitude of curiosity, see whether you notice any sensations in your shins or calf muscles. Can you feel your pants or socks touching your skin? Do you notice pulsations or tingles in your legs? Can you notice the muscles in your legs? Begin to imagine your breath moving in and out through your calf muscles, and with each in-breath sharpen your focus on the sensations; with each out-breath release tightness and tension. If your mind wanders, see whether you are able to notice that your attention has shifted, without judging yourself. You are seeing the nature of your mind at its most clear and natural when you observe the way your mind shifts, producing thoughts moving from one topic to the next. Bring your attention back to the sensations in your lower legs. After a minute or so, move your attention to your upper legs, your thighs. Again notice whatever sensations are present, and if it is helpful, imagine your breathing moving in and out through the muscles of your thighs, releasing tightness and tension as you exhale, focusing your awareness as you inhale. Continue moving slowly up the body in this manner, spending a few minutes on various body parts. After your upper legs, you can notice your

hands on your lap, your arms, your back and shoulders, your neck, your jaw, the muscles around your eyes, and your forehead. Depending on how much time you wish to spend meditating, you can visit fewer or more places, spending just a few minutes at each spot, breathing in and out and noticing the sensations. Before you finish, take a few moments to slowly scan your awareness through your body from head to toe. If you notice any areas of tightness or tension, let your awareness settle there for a few moments, breathing in and out through that tight place, and observing the sensations there. And again, when you notice your mind has wandered, just observe that. Allow yourself to be a curious scientist learning about how thoughts flow, rather than a punitive prison guard flogging yourself for moving outside the box. Finally, settle your attention on your breath, watching the sensations as you take two or three slow, deep breaths before opening your eyes. Take a few moments to stretch in any way that feels comfortable before getting up.

(Rogers, 2016, pp. 38–39)

This type of meditation helps place setbacks in perspective. "Fall seven times, rise eight" is a popular Japanese proverb suggesting that even during times of deep uncertainty or challenge, it is possible to function and even flourish. "Anyone can be cooperative, patient, and understanding when things are going well and life is good. But it is the noble person who can behave with grace and compassion and even kindness when times are very, very bad" (Reynolds, 2011, p. 1). Practicing this outlook can help nurture a growth mindset and grit, convincing music teachers and their students that progress can still be made, even during times of uncertainty. A fixed mindset will result in stagnation and frustration, but a growth mindset and grit will allow for deep levels of perseverance and resilience (e.g., Duckworth, 2016; Dweck, 2007).

Revisiting the music student, Ari, from the beginning of this chapter, let's consider how their life would be improved with healthy levels of resilience in the face of challenges. Ari still identifies as gender non-binary and feels generally accepted by peers at the university. But instead of leaving the situation at that, Ari joins a support group at the beginning of their freshman year and meets other students in similar situations. In fact, instead of considering the non-binary feelings as a challenge or deficit, Ari learns to embrace and celebrate their life. This renewed viewpoint leaves Ari feeling stronger and more resilient, providing confidence for more proactive conversations with their mother. Ari learns of another support group in their hometown and invites their mother to attend. Mom is hesitant at first but joins meetings on occasion and gradually gets to know other participants and their families. Acceptance is not immediate, and there is still work to be done, but Ari feels so much stronger and more supported by their mother by the middle of freshman year.

This strength and grounding leads Ari to join a related mindfulness group on campus. Ari learns techniques and strategies for grounding themself during challenging situations and employs these during teaching field experiences. Ari stands tall and proud on the podium while leading band warm-ups in their new pantsuit. When they notice a percussionist smirking in the back of the room, they employ curiosity about the situation. "Is everything okay?" they ask the young boy. "Um, what?" he responds. The middle schooler is surprised that a teacher would even notice him as an uncomfortable percussionist in the back of the room. "I don't really know what's going on," he mumbles. "Am I supposed to be on mallets?" Ari smiles warmly and confirms that the student should take nearby mallets for the multi-octave marimba. "Remember what we discussed about hand positioning and join your friend over there." The student nods, and Ari confidently returns to rehearsing the full band. Ari's field supervisor is impressed and writes, "A natural fit for Music Education!" on Ari's assessment form for the day. Ari uses this success to be even more determined about their music theory classes. While there are still struggles in this setting, Ari recognizes their strengths and weaknesses and remains convinced that some progress can be made. By the time Ari reaches student teaching, music theory is still a little uncomfortable, but the challenge makes Ari a great success for carefully explaining chord analysis and modulations to a group of struggling high school students. They obviously respect "Mx. Ari" and value their teaching.

Summary

- Position well for rebounds.
- Be aware of personal learning styles, motivations, and potential biases.
- Practice self-care, organize time, and protect against overload of responsibilities.
- Consider the perspectives of others, both personally and culturally.
- Make a plan for the future. Writing ideas and brainstorming with others can help.
- Practice mindfulness, both formally and informally.
- Develop and maintain grit, even in the face of difficult challenges.
- Practice growth mindset, maintaining confidence that learning can be lifelong.
- Practice gratitude to remember all that is well.
- Accept "failure" as a natural process, knowing that rebounds are possible.
- Fall seven times, rise eight.

References

Aguilar, E. (2018). *Onward: Cultivating emotional resilience in educators*. John Wiley & Sons.
Carr, A. (2020). *Positive psychology and you: A self-development guide*. Routledge.
Clear, J. (2018). *Atomic habits: An easy and proven way to build good habits and break bad ones*. Avery.
Davidson, R. (2012). *The emotional life of your brain*. Penguin.
Duckworth, A. (2016). *Grit: The power of passion and perseverance*. Scribner.
Duhigg, C. (2014). *The power of habit: Why we do what we do in life and in business*. Random House.
Dweck, C. S. (2007). *Mindset: The new psychology of success*. Ballentine Books.
Goodall, J., Abrams, D., & Hudson, G. (2021). *The book of hope: A survival guide for trying times*. Celadon Books.
Harris, B. (2020). *17 things resilient teachers do*. Routledge.
Hawkins, K. (2017). *Mindful teacher, mindful school: Improving wellbeing in teaching and learning*. Sage.
Holiday, R., & Hanselman, S. (2016). *The daily stoic: 366 meditations on wisdom, perseverance, and the art of living*. Profile Books.
Jennings, P. A. (2015). *Mindfulness for teachers: Simple skills for peace and productivity in the classroom*. Norton.
Jennings, P. A. (2021). *Teacher burnout turnaround: Strategies for empowered educators*. Norton.
King, V., & Huppert, F. (2021). Foundations for a brighter future. In B. Grenville-Cleave, D. Guomundsdottir, F. Huppert, V. King, D. Roffey, S. Roffey, & M. de Vries (Eds.), *Creating the world we want to live in: How positive psychology can build a brighter future* (pp. 3–19). Routledge.
Powell, B., & Burstein, S. (2017). Popular music and modern band principles. In G. D. Smith, Z. Moir, M. Brennan, S. Rambarran, & P. Kirkman (Eds.), *The Routledge research companion to popular music education* (pp. 243–254). Routledge.
Reynolds, G. (2011). *Fall down seven times, get up eight: The power of Japanese resilience*. Retrieved January 15, 2022, from www.presentationzen.com/presentationzen/2011/03/fall-down-seven-times-get-up-eight-the-power-of-japanese-resilience.html
Rogers, H. B. (2016). *The mindful twenty-something: Life skills to handle stress and everything else*. New Harbinger Publications.
Seligman, M. E. P. (2018). *The hope circuit: A psychologist's journey from helplessness to optimism*. Public Affairs.
Srinivasan, M. (2014). *Teach, breathe, learn: Mindfulness in and out of the classroom*. Parallax Press.
Wood, G. W. (2021). *The psychology of wellbeing*. Routledge.

8 Hope

Erik sighs a shallow breath of annoyance, lamenting another show choir season lost to the pandemic. While his administrators recently approved a shift back to in-person singing, they're requiring face coverings for everyone and at least six feet of distance between each student, rendering any kind of traditional choreography impossible. Erik hasn't communicated with his administrators since the beginning of the pandemic, simply accepting their decisions as his doomed fate. He is disappointed by the poor quality of vocal technique when his students try to sing, as they lack sufficient independent musicianship to confidently produce through fabric at a distance.

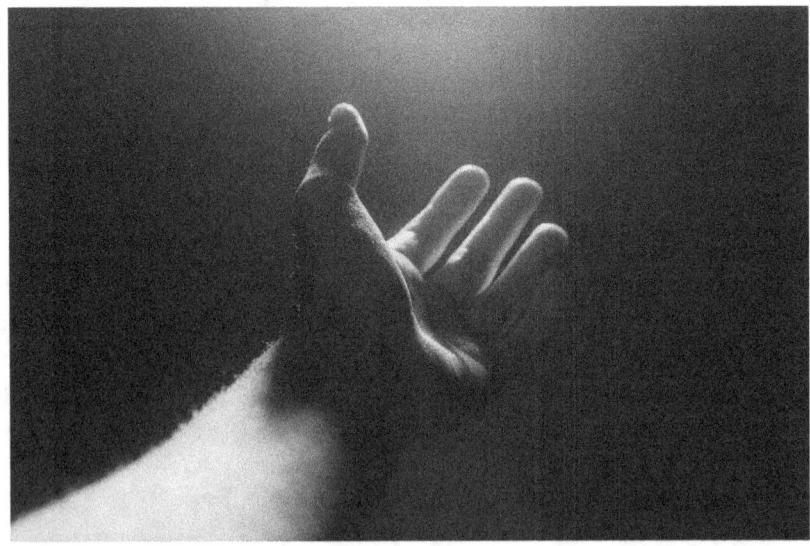

DOI: 10.4324/9781003331148-8

Instead of working through the challenge or even seeking opportunities in the new environment, Erik yells at his students and insists that silent study hall will continue through the remainder of the school year.

Adding to these frustrations, Erik is concerned about looming personal student loan payments, with upcoming monthly increases that are financially out of his reach. Erik has maxed out several credit cards and committed to long-term leases on upscale living quarters and vehicles, all while ignoring the reality that this day would soon arrive. "I could have handled all of this without the pandemic," Erik wrongfully assumes, "but the world is just crashing down around me, and everything feels hopeless." All of Erik's negativity, professional and personal, also impacts his ability to maintain relationships. His boyfriend of several years has recently moved on, and Erik has been ghosted by several blind dates. Erik's students are frustrated by his sour outlook and lack of engagement, losing respect and complaining to administrators about their formerly beloved show choir director. By the end of the school year, enrollment in the ensemble has plummeted by more than two-thirds.

Erik longs for his past, struggles with coping mechanisms for his present, and certainly lacks any hope for his future. Like some others in music education, he has learned and is demonstrating a certain sense of helplessness. Seligman (2018) studied learned helplessness early in his career and discovered that dogs exposed to mild shock treatment gradually adapted to the negative stimulus and often gave up any attempt for escape. Similarly, many humans experience trauma, both mild and severe, that gradually leads to feelings of despair and depression (Seligman, 2018). For many music teachers and education majors, the COVID-19 pandemic caused unexpected challenges, sometimes to the point of despair-inducing trauma. Educators like Erik were forced to teach via online platforms, attempting to repair and tune instruments, connect with students, and teach music content in near-impossible settings. When returning in-person teaching, many were not permitted to teach music content due to related health restrictions and were sometimes shifted to other subjects or even removed from their jobs. While the situation gradually improved for most, music teachers are still battling to maintain or build lost student enrollment and are seeking ways to reestablish previously successful practices or evolve to something new and better.

Some music education majors, or pre-service teachers, also experienced and continue to struggle with feelings of helplessness. Student teachers during the spring of 2020 lost most of their formal field experience and entered the profession with emergency or temporary teaching certification. Those starting or in the midst of undergraduate programs experienced significant portions of coursework via Zoom and other online platforms. Conducting live ensembles, performing with others, and early field experiences were all placed on hold. Even as some limitations have been lifted, many of these candidates continue to struggle.

Despite these challenges, numerous authors offer reason for optimism (e.g., Goodall et al., 2021; Gwinn & Hellman, 2019; Lopez, 2014; Seligman, 2018). They suggest that practices related to hope can turn the tide of negativity and, while still involving concentrated effort, provide direction and clarity for current resolve and future progress. "Hope is what enables us to keep going in the face of adversity. It is what we desire to happen, but we must be prepared to work hard to make it so" (Goodall et al., 2021, p. 8). In a meta-analysis, Lopez (2014) demonstrated that hope can positively impact academic achievement, workplace success, physical health, and overall happiness. Similarly, Day et al. (2010) found that hope was a better predictor of academic success than intelligence, personality, or prior achievement, while Reichard et al. (2013) found that hope predicts 14% of workplace productivity, more important than intelligence or optimism.

While attention to the present is important, Seligman (2018) suggested that human beings have a unique ability to plan for the future, employing the term "prospection" (p. 349). Without creating undue anxiety or catastrophizing about negative possibilities, it is important to imagine positive outcomes for the future. Projecting possible paths and goals creates space for opportunity and growth.

> Traditional psychology tells us that we are creatures of the past and the present, . . . but I believe that the unrivaled human ability of imagining futures uniquely describes our species, . . . and this ability might ultimately make the aspiration of wisdom a reality.
> (Seligman, 2018, pp. 349–350)

Seligman and colleagues used a self-report test, the Attributional Style Questionnaire (Peterson et al., 1982; Sweeney et al., 1986), to investigate the optimism, pessimism, and performance of Olympic swimmers, professional basketball teams, and insurance salespeople. In all three studies, the researchers found that participants reporting high levels of optimism versus pessimism (internal, stable, and specific causes versus external, unstable, and global) improved performance after disappointing setbacks. For example, Olympic swimmers were falsely informed that they had just finished an event slightly slower than usual. In a second attempt, swimmers who reported high levels of optimism performed slightly faster than the first attempt, while pessimistic swimmers performed even slower than before (Seligman et al., 1990).

Considering these findings during the COVID-19 pandemic, there is support for recognizing silver linings and potential for the future. While none of us would purposely choose the situation again, opportunities abound for creativity, connecting via distance technology, and attention to mental care. For example, using virtual platforms to visit with guest clinicians from remote parts of the country or world can provide unique perspectives previously unavailable. Creating multitrack performances with a single performer can help students hear and better understand melody, harmony, and bass lines or perhaps improvise and compose given set parameters. And taking time to simply check in with students and colleagues, even before or after traditional classes and rehearsals, can build bridges that celebrate personal connection while also improving collegiality and respect. Even during traditional times, music educators with hope will patiently observe the occasional poor rehearsal or practice session, knowing that with careful attention, better days will come. "Hope connects us to our future dreams and aspirations. You expect the best in the future, and you work to achieve it. You believe that the future is something that you can control" (Carr, 2020, p. 37).

Despite these opportunities, caution should be exercised to consider potential underlying trauma or inequities. Practicing self-care, including self-compassion (e.g., Bernhard, 2021; Wood, 2021), and considering perspectives of others, even if details are not fully available, can help people negotiate potential pitfalls and misunderstandings. "Interestingly, more hopeful people actually anticipate setbacks along the way and work to remove them" (Goodall et al., 2021, p. 27). Amanda Gorman's poem "New Day's Lyric," shared to begin the 2022 calendar year, reminds us that while hope is important, it is not a simple matter of Pollyanna sweetness or neglect of underlying problems.

> May this be the day/ We come together./ Mourning, we come to mend,/ Withered, we come to weather,/ Torn, we come to tend,/ Battered, we come to better./ Tethered by this year of yearning,/ We are learning/ That though we weren't ready for this,/ We have been readied by it./ Steadily we vow that no matter/ How we are weighed down,/ We must always pave a way forward./ This hope is our door, our portal./ Even if we never get back to normal,/ Someday we can venture beyond it,/ To leave the known and take the first steps./ So let us not return to what was normal,/ But reach toward what is next./ What was cursed, we will cure./ What was plagued, we will prove pure./ Where we tend to argue, we will tend to agree,/ Those fortunes we forswore, now the future we foresee,/ Where we weren't aware, we're now awake;/ Those moments we missed/ Are now these moments we make,/ The moments we meet,/ And our hearts, once all together beaten,/ Now all together beat./ Come, look up with kindness yet,/ For even solace can be sourced

from sorrow./ We remember, not just for the sake of yesterday,/ But to take on tomorrow./ We heed this old spirit,/ In a new day's lyric,/ In our hearts we hear it:/ For auld lang syne, my dear,/ For auld lang syne./ Be bold, sang Time this year,/ Be bold, sang Time,/ For when you honor yesterday,/ Tomorrow ye will find./ Know what we've fought/ Need not be forgot nor for none./ It defines us, binds us as one,/ Come over, join this day just begun./ For wherever we come together,/ We will forever overcome./ End.

(Gorman, 2021)

Recommendations for Practicing Hope

Goodall et al. (2021) stated four components needed for hope: goals, pathways, confidence, and support. Goals can help music educators consider short- and long-term plans for the future. A long-term goal might be something like making space for more creativity in classes and rehearsals. Short-term goals might include implementing a rotating-seating plan for the next concert cycle. Pathways are routes to follow toward goal fulfillment. For both aforementioned goals, attendance at conference sessions and observation of other successful music programs might aid in motivation and implementation. Confidence can be challenging at first but will grow exponentially with every success (see Chapter 6). Confidence is also more likely with sound attention to personal health: sleep, physical movement, and nutrition. Support can come from a variety of sources, including self-motivation, but will likely be needed from colleagues, administrators, and parents. Requesting formal meetings can help music educators share visions and goals, as can more informal conversations between classes, in school staff rooms, or beyond the traditional instructional day. "Some researchers call these four components the 'hope cycle' because the more of each we have, the more they encourage each other and inspire hope in our life" (Goodall et al., 2021, p. 30).

Create a vision board to assist with goal setting and planning. This could be an individual project or a group effort, and there is no one way to go about it. Using a list of goals for the future, draw, photograph, or source images from places like newspapers and magazines. Take some quiet time to imagine how the images might be presented for aesthetic appeal and visual motivation. Final projects could be digital or prepared on surfaces such as corkboard or magnetic whiteboard (Regan, 2021). While this might seem a childlike activity or similar to a bulletin board found in an elementary school, the process and final product can be helpful in thinking through hopeful scenarios. Possible directions for music educators might include self-care, new curricular directions for classes and ensembles, and potential changes in career trajectory.

Learn from younger colleagues, peers, and students. Don't assume that older always means wiser. Describing her reasons for hope during trying times, Jane Goodall included the power of young people. While shunning the notion that we should simply ignore current challenges to let a younger generation later grapple with them, she encouraged more experienced teachers and leaders to work cooperatively with younger colleagues and students (Goodall et al., 2021). A friend of mine recently told an interesting story from her experiences as a high school orchestra teacher. One of her students would arrive before school every morning and play by ear from the rehearsal room piano. My friend, his teacher, would remind the student that anyone arriving early to school should remain quiet and use the time for study. When the student kept slyly returning to the piano, the teacher finally visited with him one morning, pulling a chair next to his spot. "Tell me more about what you're doing," she said. The student explained that he played gospel music at his church and wanted to do more of that style at school. Another month of conversation led to the establishment of an extracurricular gospel choir at the high school. My friend taught orchestra at two other schools and thus didn't have room in her schedule to lead the group, but the student, a senior at the school, proudly took the helm and taught her and others at the school more than they could possibly imagine.

Similarly, community efforts are important to hope.

> It is important to take action and realize that we *can* make a difference, and this will encourage others to take action, and then we realize we are not alone and our cumulative actions truly make an even greater difference. This is how we spread the light. And this, of course, makes us all ever more hopeful.
>
> (Goodall et al., 2021, p. 29)

de Vries (2021) agreed, stating the importance of collective action: "For most of us, community is a vehicle for addressing the positive psychology principles of connection, positive feelings, and meaning" (p. 125). Abramowitz (2005) compared responses of Guinean communities recovering from violent military conflict. While all communities suffered trauma, those that practiced reciprocity, charity, and shared stories of hope recovered more healthily than those that fell into internal conflict and blame.

> During times of complexity and uncertainty, too much agreement and too much polarization are not healthy. An important lesson that we humans need to learn is to harness our conflict rather than suppress it.

> We need to learn how to engage in questioning and disagreement safely so that we can try out multiple perspectives and alternatives.
>
> (Jennings, 2021, p. 89)

As we recover from the COVID-19 pandemic and continue traditional forms of music advocacy, we must embrace one another and build coalitions of various stakeholders. It is important, and indeed essential, to have productive conversations with administrators and politicians and to be afforded autonomy at the local level. Music educators must be properly compensated and music programs properly funded. Continuing education must be offered and encouraged. Space for open conversation must be provided, and teachers must be trusted.

> Positive community appraisal of a situation is linked to maintaining a focus on community assets, strengths, skills and history to mobilize individuals and promote flourishing. Sharing realistic stories can create understanding and offer fresh points of view facilitating social agency. Community leaders play an important role by stimulating participation and modeling desirable roles, as well as being open to a range of perspectives. The immediate feedback of people's participation in community life can open avenues of hope and optimism, spurring the community into positive action.
>
> (de Vries, 2021, p. 133)

Revisiting the music teacher, Erik, from the beginning of this chapter, let's consider how his life would be improved with healthy levels of hope for the future. While traditional show choir choreography, performance, and competitive travel are still off limits due to the pandemic, Erik proactively and regularly meets with his administrators to discuss options. While they want to help, they provide space and autonomy for Erik to make decisions that are best for his program. The administrative budget remains a challenge, but Erik's leaders find a small sum of money for him to attend a couple of online conferences, where he exchanges ideas with other music teachers and learns about further free resources. One of the sessions he attends motivates Erik to try song writing with his students. After negotiating with his administrators and checking with other schools, Erik receives permission to reduce physical distancing to three feet while still requiring all participants to be masked. However, instead of being stymied, the students embrace opportunities to write lyrics and create music related to the current environment. Erik teams up with English teachers and counselors from his school, who help students express powerful emotions about past experiences, current situations, and future dreams. While a live traditional concert is still not permitted by district policies, Erik helps (and learns from) students to create digital versions of their creations for sharing via approved social media and the school website. Some of the students still miss show choir, but Erik must admit that he has never witnessed such strong motivation and enthusiastic participation in the program.

Erik's mood and hope for the future are further boosted by recent good news about his student loans. After meeting with a district-provided financial advisor through his school's human resources office, Erik learns that he can reconsolidate some of his loans to lower the cumulative monthly payment. He agrees to let one of his vehicles go and is able to downsize to a more modest condominium for the upcoming year. While Erik is a tad disappointed by these moves, he admits that less is more in terms of attention and focus at home and at work. Erik also notices students and other acquaintances treating him with more respect and openness. Erik is encouraged by a new personal relationship and hopes that the man will consider moving in with him as he shifts to new living quarters.

Summary

- List current concerns and challenges. Writing with pen and paper can help you process.
- Consider why these might be happening. Which are within or beyond your control?
- Consider whether the concerns and challenges are real or manifestations of the mind.
- List realistic goals for the immediate and long-term future.
- Create a vision board. Choose pictures and other items that represent a hopeful future.
- Meet with friends and colleagues to exchange ideas about concerns and hopes.
- Allow yourself to be vulnerable with a few close relationships. Build deep levels of trust.
- Remain curious, yet emotionally stable, with others. Listen with full intent.
- Learn from younger colleagues and students. Don't assume that older always means wiser.
- Seek formal meetings with administrators and other leaders. Negotiate a manageable plan for the future.
- Practice breathing meditation while focusing on desired outcomes.
- Remain calm when setbacks occur. Practice gratitude and remember what is going well.

Epilogue

Erik is feeling some relief as pandemic restrictions gradually ease and his school returns to a somewhat sense of normal. But instead of jumping back full force into show choir activities, he shifts that ensemble to only one period per day for the few students with interest and focuses more on offerings that will encourage the entire school population to participate in music. To help those efforts, Erik attends an in-person state music education conference, the first of its kind since before the pandemic began, and notices the impressive energy and collegiality upon his arrival. While standing in line at the registration area, he notices a trio of music educators chatting about instrument brands and curricula. While he would normally turn away from such topics, he's intrigued by the combination of participants. Two appear to be fairly young, and are both proudly sporting collegiate state music education pins, while the third of their group appears to be a bit older. He introduces himself as Harry and is excited to learn that Olivia and Ari are saxophone and horn majors, respectively. He offers to have them observe and do some field teaching at his high school, and they all enthusiastically exchange ideas about reconsidering traditional concert band offerings in a post-pandemic world. Later, Erik attends a fantastic session about song writing with digital audio workstations and is introduced to Randi, Nathaniel, and Patricia. They teach a variety of age levels, and their ideas about choral and general music curricula inspire Erik to try some new techniques with his choirs and other students upon return from the conference.

These seven music educators are just a small example of what might be possible during a post-pandemic period of growth and renewal. While none of us would choose to relive the many days, weeks, months, and years of COVID-19 challenges, it is possible to learn and change for the better by studying lessons from positive psychology. Serious issues should be addressed by a medical professional, and initial attention should be given to healthy sleep, physical movement, and nutrition. But by then embracing concepts of positive emotion, engagement, relationships, meaning, accomplishment, resilience, and hope, we can make space for conversation and creativity as we celebrate traditions while forging new directions in music education.

References

Abramowitz, S. A. (2005). The poor have become rich, and the rich have become poor: Collective trauma in the Guinean Languette. *Social Science & Medicine*, *61*(10), 2106–2118.

Bernhard, H. C. (2021). *Managing stress in music education: Routes to wellness and vitality*. Routledge.

Carr, A. (2020). *Positive psychology and you: A self-development guide.* Routledge.
Day, L., Hanson, K., Maltby, J., Proctor, C., & Wood, A. (2010). Hope uniquely predicts objective academic achievement above intelligence, personality, and previous academic achievement. *Journal of Research in Personality, 44*(4), 550–553.
de Vries, M. (2021). Community. In B. Grenville-Cleave, D. Guomundsdottir, F. Huppert, V. King, D. Roffey, S. Roffey, & M. de Vries (Eds.), *Creating the world we want to live in: How positive psychology can build a brighter future* (pp. 125–140). Routledge.
Goodall, J., Abrams, D., & Hudson, G. (2021). *The book of hope: A survival guide for trying times.* Celadon Books.
Gorman, A. (2021). *New year's lyric.* Retrieved January 4, 2022, from https://apnews.com/article/entertainment-lifestyle-amanda-gorman-arts-and-entertainment-7dd183a6a13c7331110cff2affe4cc40
Gwinn, C., & Hellman, C. (2019). *Hope rising: How the science of HOPE can change your life.* Morgan James.
Jennings, P. A. (2021). *Teacher burnout turnaround: Strategies for empowered educators.* Norton.
Lopez, S. (2014). *Making hope happen: Creating the future you want for yourself and others.* Atria.
Peterson, C., Semmel, A., von Baeyer, C., Abramson, L. T., Metalsky, G. I., & Seligman, M. E. P. (1982). The attributional style questionnaire. *Cognitive Therapy and Research, 6*, 287–300.
Regan, S. (2021). *How vision boards work and how to make a powerful one for yourself.* Retrieved January 7, 2022, from www.mindbodygreen.com/articles/how-to-make-a-vision-board
Reichard, R. J., Avey, J. B., Lopez, S., & Dollwet, M. (2013). Having the will and finding the way: A review and meta-analysis of hope at work. *The Journal of Positive Psychology, 8*(4), 292–304.
Seligman, M. E. P. (2018). *The hope circuit: A psychologist's journey from helplessness to optimism.* Public Affairs.
Seligman, M. E. P., Nolen-Hoeksema, S., Thornton, N., & Thornton, K. M. (1990). Explanatory style as a mechanism of disappointing athletic performance. *Psychological Science, 1*, 143–146.
Sweeney, P. D., Anderson, K., & Bailey, S. (1986). Attributional style in depression: A meta-analytic review. *Journal of Personality and Social Psychology, 50*, 974–991.
Wood, G. W. (2021). *The psychology of wellbeing.* Routledge.

Index

academic achievement, hope (impact) 70
academic success, predictor 70
acceptance, struggle 30
accomplishment 3, 5, 49; environment, creation/impact 55; feelings 52; habits, stacking 53–54; recognition, recommendations 53–56
adaptation, importance 61
administrative directives, impact 14
administrators, communication (absence) 68
adrenaline rush 8
adversity, adaptive coping 52
aerobic activity, usage 4
agreeableness, relationships (connection) 52
annoyances, reframing 13
anxiety, feelings 20
anxious attachment style, negotiation 34–35
appreciable goals 44
Aristuppus 10
attachment theory 30–31
attention deficit hyperactivity disorder, impact 49
Attributional Style Questionnaire, usage 70
auditioning 8
autonomy 14; perception 22; providing 74–75; seeking 44
avoidant attachment style, negotiation 34–35
awareness: maintenance 54–55; practice 64–65
awe (positive emotion component) 14

behavior, connection 54
biological/psychological functioning, sleep (importance) 3–4
blood pressure, reduction 11
blue emotional system 34
body scan meditation, usage 5
boredom, embracing 21
brainstorming 23
breath, attention/focus 32, 64
breathing, practice 5, 15
Buddhism, impact 5
Buffett, Warren (career successes) 44–45
burnout, construct (study) 51
busyness, obsession 25

capitalizing, involvement 34
career achievements 42
career trajectories 40–41; brainstorming 44; changes 72
character strengths, identification 41
charity, practice 73
childhood/parent interactions, fulfillment 30–31
Clance Impostor Phenomenon Scale 52
click bait, impact 20
closeness, invitations (resistance) 31
collaborative goals 44
colleagues, goals (differences) 44
collective creativity 22
collegiality, improvement 71
comments, importance (minimization) 36
communication, struggles 28
community leaders, role (importance) 74
compassion, roots 32
confidence: high levels, problem 52–53; hope component 72

connection: positive psychological principles 73; recommendations 32–36
conscientiousness, relationships (connection) 52
consciousness, requirement 13
contempt 32
contingency plans, making 62–63
conversation, engagement 60
coping mechanisms, struggle 69
COVID-19 pandemic: distraction, challenge 20–21; happiness/gratitude levels, comparison 3; impact 51–52, 69; isolation, increase 30; music educators, challenges 2, 4–5; pleasure, self-reported levels (increase) 10; recovery 74; self-reported psychological meaning, strength 41
creativity: multidimensional model 22; process, savoring/engagement (impact) 22
criticism 32
curiosity, practice 14

deep focus, avoidance (excuse) 22
deep listening, usage 24
defensiveness 32
dependency levels (problem) 22–23
depersonalization 51
depression, feelings 69
descriptors, usage 54
despair, feelings 69
difficult people, visualization 33
disagreement, engagement (learning) 74
discovery, enhancement 22
disruptions, identification 23
distraction: challenge 20–21; levels, problems 22–23
distress, relief 11

"eating that frog" concept 24
economic struggle 20
emails, impact 23
emotional exhaustion 51
emotional goals 44
emotional highs, chasing 10
emotional stability 35; relationships, connection 52
emotional support, absence 31

emotions, regulation (theory) 34
empathic creativity 22
empathy, demonstration 61
endorphins, importance 30
engagement 18; additive quality 3; impact 22; occurrence 19–20; scores 21
environment: control, impact 42–43; creation 55
extraversion, relationships (connection) 52

fairness, scores (indications) 41–42
family/friends, relationships 42
fatigue, creation 35–36
feedback, requirements 35
fight or flight reactions, protection 63
flow (Csikszentmihalyi) 19
focus, maintenance (difficulty) 55
formal meditation: basics, learning 15; limitations 64
formal mindfulness, usage 64
free time, usage (determination) 42–43
frustrations 69

goals: attainment 63; hope component 72; list/types, usage 44; setting, vision board (creation) 72
Goodall, Jane 60–61, 73
Gorman, Amanda 71
gratitude: cores 21; importance 13–14; practice 13; return 15; scores, indications 41–42; usefulness 11–12
green emotional system 34
grit (psychological trait) 62
growth mindset: occurrence 61–62; resilience, connection 62
growth optimism, maintenance 41–42
guilt, feelings 23–24, 39–40

happiness: hope, impact 70; levels, gratitude levels (comparison) 3; psychological engagement, relationship 5–6
hedonism, doctrine 10
hedonistic pleasure, examples 10
helplessness, feelings (struggle) 69–70
high school concert band rehearsal 8–9
hope 68; boost 75; components 72; description, writing 42; impact 70;

Index

practice, recommendations 72–75; scores, indications 41–42; shared stories, practice 73
hopelessness, feelings 69
human connection: importance 31; struggle 28
humans: emotions, regulation systems 34; flourishing, PERMA model 51; interactions, involvement 62–63; relationships, negotiation 30, 36; resilience 61; spirit 61
humor, scores (indications) 41–42
hygge (warmth/comfort awareness) 13

ikigai 45
immunity, increase 11
imposter syndrome 52
Industrial Revolution, education practices 2
inequities, issues (consideration) 71
informal meditation, basics (learning) 15
informal mindfulness: practice 64; usage 25
information overload 22–23
insecure attachment styles, negotiation 34–35
intensity, increase 19–20
interests, brainstorming 44
intrinsic motivation, difficulty 42–43
invention, enhancement 22
isolation, feelings 30; reduction 11–12

job satisfaction, improvement 52
joy (positive emotion component) 14

kindness 65; acts, impact 33–34; demonstration 61; extension 33; importance 12; maintenance 54–55
Koch, Chris 61

leadership, scores (indications) 41–42
learned helplessness, study 2–3
learning: improvement 24; loss 20; styles, study 63
leisure: activities, psychological meaning (consideration) 43; time, meaning (search) 45
lesson plan, writing 18–19
life: control, loss 44–45; enjoyment 36; improvement 55–56; meaning, finding (ikigai) 45; meaning,
goals (differences) 44; tailwinds/headwinds, recognition 11
life meaning: additive quality 3; importance 10
lifestyles, health (improvement) 52
limited goals 44
loneliness, feelings (reduction) 11–12
love, visualization 32
loving-kindness meditation 32–34; roots 32

Managing Stress in Music Education (Bernhard) 3–6, 32
Maslach, Christina 2, 51
meaning 39; positive psychological principles 732; scores 21
meditation: basics, learning 15; roots 32
memories, power 21–22
menial tasks, identification 23
mental deficiencies, study 2–3
mental health 42; improvement 15, 42–43
mental space, importance 12
micronutrients/macronutrients, balance 4
mindful awareness 61–62
mindful exercise, usage 25
mindfulness: activities 32–33; group, joining 66; practice, impact 24; usage 5, 61, 64
mood, improvement 75; physical movement, impact 54
multitasking: avoidance 45; usage 39–40
multitrack performances, creation 71
music advocacy, continuation 74
music education profession: control, loss 44–45; systemic change, argument 2
music educators: pandemic challenge 2; people-pleasers 23–24; self-advocacy 43
musicianship: development, stunting 10; improvement 24; understanding 49
music teachers: inferiority, sense 2; mindfulness practice 24; overload 13; volunteering, benefits 34
music, teaching (messiness/complexity) 62–63
music theory classes, struggle 60

naturalness bias 62
negative thoughts, changes 11

negativity, feelings 32
nervousness, feelings 20
"New Day's Lyric" (Gorman) 71–72
non-binary feelings, consideration 65–66
not-to-do list, making 23
nurturing, experience 30–31
nutrition, importance 4, 13

openness, increase 75
optimism: learning 43; maintenance 41–42; pessimism, contrast 70; reasons (Goodall) 60; reasons, offering 70

parents, relationships (building/maintaining) 35
participation, development (excuses/absence) 32
partners, relationships 42
pathways (hope component) 72
patience: exercise 21–22; requirement 21
performances: denigration 50–51; improvement 70; overestimation/underestimation 53
PERMA model 51
PERMA profiler, usage 51–52
perseverance 65
personal accomplishments, additive quality 3
personal accomplishments, recognition: importance 53; low level 51
personal contexts, accomplishments (celebration) 55
perspective, scores (indications) 41–42
physical activity 42–43
physical distancing, reduction (permission) 74–75
physical health 42; hope, impact 70
physical movement: impact 54; importance 4, 13
planning, vision board (creation) 72
plans, description 42
pleasure: psychological principle, study 11; self-reported levels, increase 10
political mandates, impact 14
positive community appraisal, usage 74
positive emotion 8; additive quality 3; benefits 11; components 14; increase 11, 13–14; opportunities 13; physical movement, impact 4; pleasure, connection 10; psychological enjoyment 10; recommendations 12–15; reflection, importance 12; removal, feeling 14; tailwinds, recognition (impact) 11; value 12
positive feelings, positive psychological principles 73
positive momentum, impact 25
positive psychology 4–5, 24, 51
praise, usage 55–56
pre-service music teachers, inferiority (sense) 2
pride, positive source 54
procrastination, anxiety (decrease) 25
productivity: improvement, physical movement (impact) 54; obsession 25
professional time, meaning (search) 45
program advocacy, positive source 54
prospection 70
psychological defense systems, broadening/building 11
psychological engagement: ability 19; concentration, deterioration 20; email/text messaging, impact 23; importance 10; improvement, patience (impact) 21–22; levels, reduction 21; patience, requirement 21; recommendations 22–26
psychological flow: extension 22; increase 25; occurrence 19–20
psychological grit 61–62
psychological meaning 40–41; derivation 42; importance 43; recommendations 43–46; self-reported psychological meaning, strength 41
psychological pleasure, impact 10
psychological well-being 53

questioning, engagement (learning) 74
quiet spaces, supply 35–36

reciprocity, practice 73
red emotional system 34
refinable goals 44
relationships 28; additive quality 3; building/maintaining 35; challenges 31–32, 35; characteristics 31; labeling 31; recommendations 32–36; self-relationship, health (importance) 30; skills, improvement 63
resilience 59; adaptation, importance 61; building, recommendations

62–66; development 36; development, mindfulness (usage) 61; encouragement, growth mindset (impact) 62; examples 60–61; growth mindset, connection 62
respect: improvement 19, 25, 71; increase 75
responsibility, freedom (benefits) 14

savoring, impact 22
schools: accomplishments, celebration 55; four-day weekend announcement 1
screen time, reduction 23
security, need 31
self, attention (achievement) 31
self-awareness, impact 63
self-esteem, struggle 30
self-management, usage 63
self-recognition, balance (achievement) 53
self-regulation, freedom (benefits) 14
self-reported psychological meaning, strength 41
self-report test, usage 70
Seligman, Martin 51
sensory gratification 10
service music teachers, inferiority (sense) 2
service, pace (deceleration) 46
setbacks, disappointment 70
short-term energy, physical movement (impact) 4
sleep: importance 3–4, 13; quality, improvement 11, 36
social awareness, involvement 63
social dysfunction 20
social life, problem 28
social media: information overload 22–23; usage 30
"space and grace" 6
space, providing 74–75
specials teacher, lesson plan (writing) 18–19
stakeholders, coalitions (building) 74
stonewalling 32
stranger, visualization 32–33
strength training, usage 4
stress: adaptive coping 52; creation 35–36; impact 63

stress, reduction 11; course, mindfulness basis 25
students: diversity, awareness/respect 31; enrollment losses, rebuilding 69; goals, differences 44; leaders, rotation (identification) 22; performances, denigration 50–51
students, relationships: building/ maintaining 35; importance 31–32
success: habits, stacking 53–54; wealth, impact 52
support, hope component 72

tasks, prioritization 24
teachers: improvements 63; political mandates/administrative directives, impact 14; responsibility 21; stress/burnout 2; support 63; traditional roles, negotiation 13–14
teaching: enjoyment, issues 39; improvement 24; pace, deceleration 46
teamwork, scores (indications) 41–42
text messaging, impact 23
Tonglen breathing practice 5
trauma: experience 69; issues, consideration 71

US teachers, resignation percentage (consideration) 1

values, identification 41
Values in Action Inventory of Strengths (VIA-IS): survey/analysis 42; usage 41
virtual platforms, usage 71
vision board, creation 72
visual images, usage 54
volunteering, acts (impact) 33–34

warm demander, expertise/training 63
warm-up practice session 25
welcoming/caring classroom, enabling 13–14
well-being, wealth (impact) 52
word clouds, usage 43–44
work performance, improvement 52
workplace success, hope (impact) 70

yoga, learning 15
young people, power 73

For Product Safety Concerns and Information please contact our EU representative GPSR@taylorandfrancis.com
Taylor & Francis Verlag GmbH, Kaufingerstraße 24, 80331 München, Germany